D0289714

LIMIT OF LIABILITY/ DISCLAIMER OF WARRANTY

This publication is designed to provide accurate and authoritative information in regard to the subject matters being covered. However, these materials have been prepared for informational purposes and are not legal advice. This information is not intended to create, and receipt of it does not constitute, an attorney-client relationship.

The advice and strategies contained herein may not be suitable for your situation. If legal advice or other expert assistance is required, seek the services of a competent professional. You should not act upon the information contained in this book without seeking advice from a lawyer licensed in your own state or country. This book is not tax advice. Each reader should seek advice based on the taxpayer's particular circumstances from an independent tax advisor.

While the author and publisher have used their best efforts in preparing this book, they make no representations or warranties with respect to the accuracy or completeness of the contents of this book and specifically disclaim any implied warranties of merchantability or fitness for a particular purpose.

Third-party resources referenced in this book are not under the control of the publisher, author or their agents, and the publisher and author specifically disclaim any and all responsibility for the content of any of these third-party resources. All third-party references and links are provided for the reader's convenience only. The inclusion of a link or reference in these materials does not imply any recommendation, approval or endorsement of that site or source by the publisher, author or any of their agents.

ROBIN F. BOND ESQ.

How to Negotiate A Killer Job Offer

The Job "Secret Agent" Series

*To Eve —
Here's to your
great success!
Robin Bond*

ISBN: 0615779190
ISBN 13: 9780615779195

TABLE OF CONTENTS

AUTHOR BIOGRAPHY

Robin Frye Bond, Esq. is the Principal and Founder of Transition Strategies, LLC (www.transition-strategies.com), a boutique employment law firm located in the Philadelphia, Pennsylvania area that represents employees in all aspects of workplace-related legal matters. Robin represents executives in transition, acting as their agent and helping them negotiate pay, perks and protections in both new employment contracts and severance deals. Robin also represents individuals in a wide range of legal disputes, including civil rights discrimination claims, restrictive covenant disputes, breach of contract and wage payment and collection matters. In **"How to Negotiate a Killer Job Offer"**, attorney Bond shares some of the job secrets she has used to achieve success in the negotiation of all types of employment deals for top-level executives.

Throughout her career, Robin Bond has been actively involved in more than 3,000 deal negotiations, helping her clients get what they want by providing the right advice, coaching and persuasive written materials that close complex deals in a win-win manner. Often Bond works in secret, coaching her clients behind the scenes – so that her clients are perceived as doing their negotiations on their own.

A nationally recognized attorney with substantial, wide-ranging experience as an in-house corporate counsel, a private practitioner and an entrepreneur, Robin Bond has been a contributing legal commentator for both CNN and FOX News, and has also provided on-air legal analysis for truTV's Open Court live television trial coverage. She is quoted in a variety of print and electronic media as an employment lawyer, including in the New York Times, the New York Post, the Wall Street Journal, MSNBC, Fox News Radio, Corporate Counsel magazine, Time magazine, Career Builder.com, and Monster.com.

Robin Bond is distinguished by her talent for communicating about legal issues in an understandable and accessible manner, gaining closure where it has proven elusive, and training attorneys, business executives, and other professionals in the art and skill of negotiation and deal-making.

Ms. Bond is recognized as a 2013 Pennsylvania Super Lawyer in the area of Employment Law. She has also been honored as the Top Lawyer of the Main Line for 2011 for Employment Law for Individuals, and as an Awesome Attorney in the Philadelphia Suburbs for 2010-2012. She is also active in numerous professional and civic associations, including serving on the Planning Committee for the Pennsylvania Bar Institute's Annual Employment Law Institute, on the Board of Directors of the Forum of Executive Women, and on PNC Bank's Women's Financial Services Advisory Board.

Ms. Bond is a frequent lecturer and published author on a variety of topics related to her areas of expertise, and a frequent speaker to groups in the corporate and nonprofit world. Ms. Bond earned her law degree from the University of Pittsburgh School of Law, and her B.A. in journalism, Phi Beta Kappa, from Indiana University, Bloomington, Indiana.

FOREWORD

Robin's great – Buy this book!

Mark Cuban
Billionaire Businessman, Media Entrepreneur
and Proud Owner of the Dallas Mavericks

Part I.
Starting Strong–The Intelligence

Introduction

Life is a series of negotiations. There is no getting around it. None of us is too good to negotiate. In fact, convincing other people to give us what we want is an integral part of every aspect of our daily lives and affects every relationship – those with our significant others, children, siblings, parents, neighbors, friends, co-workers and bosses.

How successful we are at negotiating can determine how happy we are with a lot of these relationships – especially our relationships at work.

Americans tend to spend an ever-increasing portion of each day on work, at work, traveling for work or with co-workers – often spending more time on-the-clock than with their families. This means that "chemistry" between co-workers, and the ability to get along well with them, is key to success on the job.

With a challenging economy, people want to find jobs with employers where they feel they have a "good fit," and where they are likely to secure employment (translation: avoid layoffs) for a long period of time.

Part of nailing the job offer is selling that "chemistry" or "good fit" component to the prospective new employer – as well as showcasing how your skills, abilities and experience are exactly what will bring the value they are seeking.

Increasingly, today's employees are all too aware that even with everything being "right" when they start a new job, there are market forces at play that can intervene and wreak havoc with their careers. Mergers, acquisitions, downsizings, rightsizings, consolidations, outsourcing, better technology, new bosses who want "their own teams," companies that run out of money – all are factors that can result in job loss due to no fault of the affected worker.

Employees can find themselves back in the unemployment line, with their families in financial peril and their careers derailed due to no fault of their own. Individuals are asking, "The next time I interview for a job, is there anything I can do to maximize not only my pay and perks, but also my protection against job loss? Can I do anything now to more easily make the transition later to my next job if this one ends up not working out?"

The answers to those questions are, in a word: "yes"– and this book is here to help you get to "yes" in obtaining the next killer job offer of your dreams.

For over thirty years, I've been an attorney and deal-maker, handling thousands of deals of all kinds –

buying and selling companies, doing commercial transactions, information technology matters, and employment contracts.

My main area of practice for over 15 years has been as an attorney who acts as an "agent for executives" – I represent individual executives in the negotiation of employment agreements when they receive new job offers and in the negotiation of enhanced severance agreements when they are exiting their prior employment situations. Once the client has the offer, we work together to negotiate final terms of that offer that are ideal for the client's needs. That usually means more pay, perks and protections.

My clients and I seek to obtain an employment contract as the way to codify the job offer terms, if possible. If not, we just work with revising the offer letters to add the enhanced terms. Flexibility and adaptability to the needs of the situation will generally get us what we need, and keep our deals moving forward.

My experience with my executive clients is fascinating. I've learned a lot. After all, it is always a highly stressful situation when facing the unknown – you do not know how a contract negotiation will end up, and the outcome of a decision you make can be six-figures or more. Understandably, people want to get these decisions right.

At this point in my career, I've worked on over 3,000 deals, and have developed a framework of how many companies handle different situations or questions that can arise in a negotiation. I've seen what's worked. I've seen what hasn't worked.

While there is no guarantee that what has been a successful negotiation strategy or tactic for someone else in the past will ever work for you with your particular employer or situation, learning from others can be illustrative and helpful as a basis upon which you can formulate the best approach to your own unique situation. Learning from the mistakes of others is also usually a good way to avoid making some very costly mistakes of your own!

Just as there are as many different job descriptions as there are jobs, there are as many different questions about job offer negotiation as there are clients. Here are some examples of common questions:

- "When do I bring up the subject of an employment contract?"
- "Is there any chance the company will pull the offer off the table if I try to negotiate?"
- "What clauses should be in my contract?"
- "How do I ask for more money?"
- "How do I value my equity in making an apples-to-apples comparison of a new offer?"
- "How do I ask for severance pay without making the company think I don't trust them?"

I often speak to groups of employees who are in transition, and facing the uncertainties of how to negotiate. I help coach these individuals on interviewing for their next jobs – and they always want to know what secrets the top executives know so that they, too, can power forward their own careers and financial futures.

Seminar attendees have asked me to share my "negotiation secrets" so that they can have an employment guide to reference for their negotiations in the future. They hope to avoid the land mines that are out there and to be successful in deal negotiations. I agree – help is needed.

These job secrets form the basis for this book. So in a way, now you can have an agent too – your own Job "Secret Agent."

Employees realize that an individual needs some level of knowledge in order to successfully "play in the big leagues." While I don't think there is a need for another 300-page negotiation book on the market, there is a definite need for a short, nuts-and-bolts, how-to employment guide that helps employees proactively negotiate a job offer.

How to Negotiate a Killer Job Offer: The Job "Secret Agent" Book Series, Volume 1, is just that. The book starts at the stage where you have already received a job offer. It teaches you how to:

- Powerfully prepare for job offer negotiations;
- Access the strategy secrets used by senior-level executives in the real world of job offer negotiations;
- Take action to maximize your chances for making the final terms of the job offer the best ones for you, and
- Successfully implement the right negotiation tactics that increase your chances of completing the mission: success.

This book is a resource to help you leverage some of the negotiation benefits that athletes, musicians and entertainers receive with the assistance of professional agents. My book is not, and cannot ever be, a guarantee that you will achieve success in any negotiation just because you read it and follow my advice. Reading any book just isn't the same thing as retaining an attorney to represent your interests in a specific job offer negotiation – which I always recommend. But getting smart about negotiation is a good thing, and my book is here to help you with that.

In **How to Negotiate a Killer Job Offer** I will outline and describe in detail the proactive negotiation process I recommend you utilize to increase your chances of obtaining the killer outcomes you desire in your next job offer.

To help you remember my proactive negotiation process and techniques, I use an acronym: AWL. Note that these are the same letters that also spell law.

Your mission, should you choose to accept it: Apply my "It's AWL About the Law" proactive negotiation techniques to your next job offer, and see if the tips from this Job "Secret Agent" don't work wonders to help you leverage the financial success you deserve. Let's get started.

Chapter 1.
Contracts and Agreements

The concept of the employment agreement dates as far back as the Ancient Roman Empire. While employment contracts have changed throughout the centuries, their central purpose has remained the same: to codify the important terms of agreement between the employee and employer in the employment relationship.

Because some type of written agreement is a desired outcome of job offer negotiations, let's get a little legal background and explore how contracts work before we jump right in to the negotiation of your new job offer.

The Elements of a Contract

An employment agreement, or contract, is defined as an agreement with specific terms between two or more people or entities in which there is a promise to do something in return for a valuable benefit known as "consideration." Employment agreements can be written or verbal. In fact, many people work under "verbal" employment arrangements, making the terms difficult to prove and enforce.

In more understandable language, this means that –a contract is an agreement between at least two parties that states, "If you do X, then I will do Y." In the employment context, this usually means, "If you do the job, I will pay you money."

Sounds simple. However, in order to fully understand how a contract works, you must first understand the basic equation of a contract and how to break down its individual key elements.

You can express a contract in a mathematical formula in this way: as an offer that gets accepted. There must be good consideration to support the exchange – something of value changing hands to form a "meeting of the minds" between the parties that makes them conclude, "Hey, we have a deal."

This formula (shown below) is Contract (K) = Offer (O) plus Acceptance (A).

$$K = O + A$$

The Offer

Let's talk about the **offer**. An offer is an expression of willingness to reach an agreement on certain terms. An offer is made with the intention that it will become a legally binding contract as soon as the other party accepts it. Offers can be made in many ways and can be as simple as:

"Hey Bob, I'll give you $20.00 to wash my car by 5:00 PM today."

In this offer, if Bob is to agree, Bob will wash the car by 5:00 PM in exchange for $20.00. There is consideration flowing both ways.

How About Some Consideration?

The offer must contain valuable consideration in order to be deemed a legal contract. The purpose of this valuable consideration, or *Quid Pro Quo* (meaning "this for that"), is to substantiate the bargain between the promisee and the promisor. The consideration in the contract can take many forms, such as money, services, physical objects, refraining from future actions or promised actions.

For example, in a typical employment contract the consideration could be as follows:

- If you do the job (X) for your employer, then you will receive (Y), an agreed upon amount of money.
- If you agree to refrain from taking a competing job post-employment (X), you will be

eligible to participate in the current employer's stock option program (Y).

As long as the consideration is something of value to the other party, it can be on the negotiation table as an item of "good consideration" to support the contract; therefore both X and Y in the above examples are potentially good consideration to support the deal.

Illusory Contracts

Remember, there must be consideration given by <u>both parties</u> in order for the contract to be valid. If only one party to the contract gives something of value, then the contract is considered an "illusory" contract and can be held unenforceable for lack of mutual consideration.

The concept of illusory contracts is particularly important in the noncompetition arena, when determining whether or not an employee actually received something of true value in exchange for signing a noncompetition agreement.

If we refer back to our example of Bob and the carwash, an illusory contract would occur in this context: "Hey Bob, I'll give you until 5:00 PM today to wash my car." Bob could rightfully say to you, "What's the consideration for me?" In this context, there is none – we can't tell that Bob is getting anything of value in exchange for washing the car. Therefore, this is not an enforceable contract.

In the noncompetition agreement scenario, the question would be: did I get something of value when I signed that noncompete agreement? In many jurisdictions that enforce noncompetes, the fact that you received an employment agreement would be sufficient consideration to support the noncompete agreement.

What does that tell us? Well, for starters, it tells us that you will for sure want to analyze the terms of your employment agreement to at least determine whether or not the severance provisions will be sufficient to help you get through any restrictive covenant time periods to which you agree. We'll go into how that negotiation process works later in this book.

Terms and "At Will" Employment

All contracts must have a start date. Contracts don't need a fixed term, or even an end date – just an effective date when the parties become legally bound by their contractual agreement.

If there is a fixed term in your contract, it means that you are required to provide your end of the bargain to the other party until the stated end date, unless the contract has early termination procedures that would let you get out of the deal – and the door - sooner.

During this fixed term, you are entitled to receive the same consideration stated in your contract throughout the duration of the term.

Sample: "Fixed Term" Contract

> *Executive's employment shall be for a three year term, commencing on _____, 201__ (the "Initial Term"). This Agreement shall not be terminable by the Employer except for Cause as defined in Paragraph __ below. This Agreement shall automatically renew and extend as provided in this paragraph 2 unless, at least sixty (60) days prior to any anniversary date of this Agreement, either the Employer or Executive gives written notice to the other of its or his intention not to extend the Agreement.*

In employment contracts, "fixed term" deals are rare – unless you are the founder of the company, or a key scientist or inventor, in which case, you may get an employment contract requiring you to commit to stay at the company for a certain term of years. This is usually done to make the company attractive for sale, or to keep the key employees on the team post-sale to ease the transition of key knowledge to the new buyers.

Most employees will have "employment at will" deal terms – meaning either they, or the employer, can terminate the employment relationship at any time with a mere minute's notice.

Sample: "At Will" Employment

It is understood that you are not being offered employment for a definite period of time and that either you or the Employer may terminate the employment relationship at any time and for any reason without prior notice. Nothing in the Employer's offer to you should be interpreted as creating a contract of employment for any specific term, or anything other than an at-will employment relationship.

At w-i-l-l should really be spelled like this: "at w-h-i-m." Then it would make more sense.

What this means is that you can come to work on time every day, work late, meet all your goals, be a team player, and then as soon as you close the biggest deal the company has ever had, the boss can come to you and say, "Gee, Jim, you've been so successful, we've decided we can put a far less skilled person in this position, so we've elected to terminate your position under the "at will" provisions of your offer letter. This means you can pack up your desk and leave now, and under the law, we don't owe you any severance, so we won't be paying any. Thank you for your service."

In Europe, jobs are more like property rights that cannot be taken away from employees without first showing "just cause" for doing so, and then paying the terminated employee a significant amount of severance pay.

In America, we went to the other extreme, where severance pay is not a legal right (but rather something management either elects to grant via a policy or for which employees have to negotiate individually or through a collective bargaining agreement).

The U.S. public policy behind the "at will" doctrine is this: states with "at will" policies believe that by having economic policies favorable to business (like "at will" employment), more employers will establish businesses in that state. This will eventually benefit everyone, because even though an individual employee who is fired without severance pay is temporarily harmed, the fact that more companies are doing business in the state will mean there are more jobs there, and the individual employee has a greater chance of finding a new job sooner.

Public policy is all well and good – for the other guy. You've probably had enough of that now and are of the belief that before your next job offer negotiation, you are certainly going to consider "severance agreement protection." I would recommend it, too. Why not enhance the odds that the "at will" public policy protection provides?

Giving Notice

What if the offer letter or company policy says you have to give two weeks' notice when terminating your job? Is that "required"? We're sidestepping a little here, but it's a question that does come up often, and I'll share this with you: If the employer has an "at will" policy that means that you, or the employer, can terminate the employment relationship at any time.

If the employer's policy requires you to give notice and says the company will pay you for the notice time, then it should do so. Many times, if you notify the employer you are leaving and going to work for a competitor, the employer will ask you to leave immediately and will stop paying you effective with your last day worked.

State laws can vary, and you'll need to check your state's law, but generally the law is that an employer only has to pay you for days worked, unless company policy says otherwise. You would call your state's Department of Labor to see if you can get assistance or get a private attorney to help you with a Wage Payment and Collection Act claim.

If you just want to leave without giving the requested two weeks' advance notice, some employers will mark your file as "not eligible for rehire," which can hurt you in the job search process. But this is variable, and I cannot say what each employer will or will not do. Most employers these days have opted for a reference practice of only giving out your dates of employment and last position held.

You may want to verify your employer's reference practices before making a decision on what notice you give before you walk out the door.

Acceptance

Once the offer has been made, it sits on the table and waits to be accepted. An acceptance results in "the meeting of the minds" that occurs when both parties reach accord. It shows the intention that the parties have to be bound by the terms and conditions set forth in the agreement.

In order to show that a written offer has been legally accepted, it needs to have the signatures of both parties, showing that they agree to the terms stated within the offer. The law says an offer has to be accepted as is, meaning you take the offer letter, sign, date, and return it, to "accept."

As discussed before, employment agreements can also be verbal, and acceptance can be as simple as picking up the phone and saying, "I accept."

Now this all seems pretty simple, right? It's like signing up for a new software program online, or agreeing to the "Terms and Conditions" of a social networking website. But what if the terms of your offer are not exactly what you dreamed of, or even worse, if they are not what you expected based upon the job interview?

In my experience, rarely will an employee receive a job offer that is 100% perfect the first time. In almost every instance, you will want to go back to negotiate about something.

This is not cause for dismay. It is an expected part of the job offer process. It is not something to be feared, but rather an opportunity to showcase the kind of executive potential you have – this is an experience to be embraced.

How to Ask Your Attorney to Help You

When I was an in-house corporate counsel, it was not unusual for me to review 50-60 contracts a month. Clients would often come to me in a rush and ask, "Robin, review this contract – we need to know if it's legally sufficient." I would say, "Well, I can tell you that in a few minutes." Here's how we tell if a contract is legally sufficient:

- Do we have an offer that is being accepted?
- Do we have consideration flowing both ways?
- Do we have an effective date or a term for the agreement?
- Do we have two competent parties signing?

Contracts I was reviewing pretty much met that test every time. What soon became apparent was that my clients didn't really want me to tell them whether or not the contract was legally sufficient. What they wanted was for me to *negotiate for them the best possible deal.*

They wanted me to expand upon the rights and responsibilities of the parties, and to rewrite the "Terms and Conditions" section of the contract to specifically tailor for each agreement just exactly what was needed in terms of obligations, expectations, and parameters for each unique situation.

They counted on me to reduce ambiguity and to try to crystalize that "meeting of the minds" so that when the parties signed each contract, they were aligned, and everyone knew what was coming next.

We all realize that you can rarely anticipate in advance and codify within a contract every possible event that can occur by and between two parties. But the ultimate goal of contract negotiations is that when you are done with the deal, both parties can just put the document away in a file drawer for reference because it is so clear from the negotiations what each is going to do and expect from each other that neither feels the need to refer to the document again.

When you work with an attorney to help you negotiate your job offer, you'll want the cursory "legal sufficiency" review; however, be sure to communicate that what you *really* want is a deal-maker. First, have the attorney analyze the offer, and tell you what is good about it, what is not so good about it, and what is missing from it.

You want the attorney to recommend how the deal could be improved and to suggest negotiation strategies to maximize the pay, benefits, and protections available to you to make this the best possible deal for you.

Finally, the attorney has to help you find the right tactics that will carry out your strategies in a winning way, convey your message, and close the deal you want. All this must be done in a way that builds rapport with your new hiring manager, does not burn any bridges, showcases your talents and abilities, and validates the company's hiring decision to make you a part of the team.

Make sure you convey this message to any attorney with whom you work so you know that you and that attorney are aligned on expectations of the engagement.

But what if you don't want to hire an attorney? What if you just want to know what an attorney would do to negotiate a better job offer? Well, if you want to know some of the secrets I have used in the job offer negotiation process to gain advantages for actual clients, read on!

Chapter 2.
Avoiding the Counteroffer Consequence

Congratulations! You have received an offer letter for employment from your desired company. You have worked hard, interviewed well, and impressed management enough for them to choose you – from a field of hundreds – to join their team.

However, before you throw a signature on that fresh offer letter, there are a few things you should consider, especially if that offer letter is not quite what you expected it to be.

Perhaps as you are reading through the letter, hot from the printer, you are thinking to yourself, *"Hmmm, there are some things in here that I'm not so sure of."*

Or, *"This document doesn't even talk about a few items that are important to me, and I'd sure like to know how the company plans to deal with them."*

Your first instinct tells you to say, "*I sure would like to accept this contract...but I would need the salary to be $5,000 higher just to stay even with the cost of living.*"

Or you might say, "*In my last job, I had four weeks of vacation, and this offer only proposes two. I wonder if there is any chance I could increase the vacation benefit to four weeks?*"

About this time, someone will say to me, "Robin, is there any chance the company will pull the offer off the table if I try to negotiate and ask for these things?" I say, "Absolutely, not. You don't have to worry. There is no chance at all that the company will pull the deal off the table."

With a skeptical look, the client will say to me, "Well, how can you be so sure?" To which, I respond, "The law tells me so." Here's what I mean.

While the above requests may sound reasonable and may even be asked quite appropriately, they do have a legal effect when negotiating. You will recall in Chapter 1 when we discussed the concept of "Acceptance," I told you that a contract is formed when you accept an offer, and you have to accept that offer "as is." If you change the terms of the offer, under the law, you are not accepting the offer, you are making a "Counteroffer." Counteroffers are made in response to a previous offer, which is thought to be unacceptable "as is"; it is a revision to the original offer in an attempt to make it more appealing.

Under the law, ***the mere utterance of a counteroffer kills the offer***. Therefore, you don't have to worry about the company pulling the offer off the table when you go back to negotiate – you do that yourself when you make a counteroffer.

The mere fact that you go back to negotiate means you kill the original offer, and once that happens, the company is under no obligation to put it back on the table again. Ever.

This is when the air goes out of the room – but only briefly. **Negotiation does have some risk.** Clients are forewarned: **there is no 100% safe way to steal second base while keeping your foot firmly planted on first base.**

However, I can tell you culturally job offers don't get pulled because you dare to ask to negotiate a few items. In all of the thousands of deals on which I have worked, I have yet to have it happen to me. Could you be the first person to whom this happens? Yes!

Why do I say that? Because the law tells me it is possible! Why do I say it's not likely to happen to you? Because the corporation hiring you has invested significant time and money to recruit talent. The result of that heroic effort is – you.

They have culled through hundreds of resumes, done phone screens, background and reference checks, done preliminary interviews, and then run the final candidates through the full, grueling interview process. The entire management team has now "bought in" to bringing you on board, and if you have a few reasonable requests, most companies will want to hear what those are, and try to meet you on them before completely throwing away all that effort just because you ask a few questions, or for a few things.

This does not mean that you can act like you are a rock star and start making crazy demands. I never recommend that – even if you are the best at what you do.

People generally do not lose deals because they ask – but they can lose deals pretty quickly because of *how* they ask. **It is our job to show the company why it should give you what you are asking for, and why giving you what you are asking for will eventually benefit the company, create value for the company, and make your boss look good.**

It's not about why you should have something "for you," of course. It's about why giving something to you is also for the good of the team, the company, and the boss. The company thinks it is offering you a job, and frankly that's pretty good in its eyes. It is up to us, as ace negotiators, to convince management to close this sale – and on the terms that are most beneficial to you. That's negotiation.

So how do we tackle a less than ideal offer and get the company to keep it on the table the entire time these deal terms are flying back and forth like ping pong balls? **A key secret of successful negotiators is that we never sound like we are making a counter-offer.** That way, we avoid dealing with the awkward situation of whether or not the offer is still on the table – we just act as if it is.

In many instances, when working with clients, I will "ghost write" a response back to the company for them, silently behind the scenes, so that the company does not know the employee is even working with an attorney.

Here are four key tactics I utilize in responding to an offer that avoids the "counteroffer consequence," and convinces the company to keep the offer alive, and the terms of the deal in discussion:

1.   Use positive words.
2.   Ask questions.
3.   Go back and clarify something discussed in the offer letter.
4.   Bring up some new matters that haven't been discussed yet.

Positive Words

We create a mood with the words we choose. You want your prospective employer's head to be nodding "yes" as he or she reads your emails. The best way to do this is through the **Power of Being Positive**. You want your future employer to think, "This candidate really wants to be here. I know that he is going to be a valuable contributor on my team."

When the hiring manager is reading my response to his job offer, I want him to "feel the love." Let's describe "feel the love" in this context: When a job offer is extended to someone, you should treat it as significantly as if it is an offer of a long-term relationship. You are entering into a type of long-term relationship, and in fact many workers say they spend more time at work than they do with their significant others.

So when you communicate with your hiring manager, you want to create the same sense of respectful communication you would with a significant other – show that hiring manager how important and meaningful he/she is to you, and how committed you are to being a part of that team, bringing value to the organization, and helping the boss.

This is the same sense of communication we strive to achieve in our response to job offer letters – respectful and "on the same team" – no more than that when I say "feel the love."

I avoid negative words like "but," "issues," "problems," "concerns," "deal-breakers," "hurdles," or "stumbling blocks." Rather, create a sense of alignment with the hiring manager, a sense that you are moving forward with the deal, and that it is only a matter of working out the small details.

Ask Questions

If there is something you do not like about the offer, or wish to improve, frame it as a question and not as a counteroffer. You are new to the company. The company fully expects you will have questions about how things work, or what benefits it offers, and will not be offended by you asking.

Questions about pay, benefits, relocation packages, work from home, car allowances, stock options, commissions – just about anything you can think of – can work here.

Clarification

Even if the company has already provided you with information about the matter in question, and you just wish to try to negotiate something different, my preferred approach is to go back and "seek clarification about a matter raised in the offer letter." Again, this is not offensive, but rather a request for information which companies expect and is typically well-received. People will listen to our positively chosen words and respond appropriately.

New Matters

Perhaps your offer letter omits something you expected but haven't had a chance to discuss yet, something like severance pay, relocation expenses, etc. This means you will have to go back to raise some new matters with the hiring manager – to bring to the company's attention something that is uncharted territory.

New matters are usually sensitive topics like severance pay, or a flexible work arrangement, or perhaps some type of accommodation for your spouse. Broaching these topics can be more delicate. Why? The company probably did not talk about them because the intent was not to give them in the first place.

My approach is not to assume this. Rather, I take the position that at the time we were talking job offer terms, you the candidate were just so focused on how to succeed in the nature of the work that you weren't really thinking about all the other terms of the job offer.

Now that you've seen the offer in writing and had some time to think about it, a few topics have crossed your mind, and out of respect for your hiring manager's time, you'd like to raise those topics in an email so you can talk about them when you two have the necessary follow-up phone call.

Hiring Manager is Key

I do recommend that your message go to your hiring manager because he or she is the one who wants you, who is committed, who has made the decision to hire you, and more importantly, who is paying for you out of his or her budget. The hiring manager is the decision-maker, and the person most motivated to find allies within the company who can and will make a deal happen with you.

If the company has said to send all responses through Human Resources, I still write to the hiring manger and also address the email to HR. But HR's role in most companies is to act as "gate-keeper," to say "No," and to keep everyone in a uniformed line. We don't want to be there.

If the company has said to send all responses through the recruiter, I still write to the hiring manger, but also address the email to the recruiter. I always tell my clients, "If you want to control your message and the meaning it conveys, then you must write it and get it directly to the person who holds the power of the purse. Then you cannot be misquoted."

The hiring manager is key – he needs to see directly what you are saying and not hear it second-hand.

Sample Response to Hiring Manager

Here's a very brief example to illustrate how these four key concepts could be applied to avoid the counteroffer consequence in a sample email response from you to a prospective new hiring manager.

In this sample, the hiring manager is reading your email, so his comments are not being shared with anyone else – they are just a likely expression of his thoughts. (I noted some of my editorial comments about the exchange as "Robin's Comments."):

You:
Dear Mr. Hiring Manager:

Thank you for the offer to join your team as the new Inside Sales Director. I look forward to hitting the ground running and helping you meet the challenging goals and objectives for this fiscal year.

Hiring Manager's response (as he reads your email:
Yes. That's good. I want that too.

You:
The offer generally looks good.

Robin's comments: I almost always say the offer looks good. Why? Because it's a job offer – how bad can it look, right? Even if I have 22 points I want to negotiate, I say it looks good – this sets the right positive tone.

Hiring Manager's response:
Head nodding up and down. "We're aligned."

You:
I just have a few questions, and out of respect for your time, I thought I would outline them in this email so that when we talk next week, we can facilitate our discussion.

Hiring Manager's response:
"Of course. You don't know the company. What are your questions? I'll get answers."

Robin's Comments: Asking questions is okay because the company expects you will not know everything about it. You are new. You don't work for this company. They expect you're going to have questions. That's okay. Ask some questions. If you don't have any questions, go back and say something like this:

You:
"Generally the offer looks good. I've reviewed it, and there are just a few points I'd like to clarify."

OR

"Generally the offer looks good but there are a few things we didn't get a chance to dis-

cuss. That's not surprising being that I was so focused on the nature of the work that I wasn't really thinking about the terms of the offer at the time. But now that I've had the time to think about it, I'd like to talk about these with you. And again, out of respect for your time, I've raised them here in this email, and we can talk about it next week."

Robin's Comments: If you respond to the company's offer in any of these ways, you do not sound like you are making a counteroffer –even though we all know you are doing so.

Why Respond in Writing?

I almost always recommend that you respond to a job offer in writing. And I'll tell you why. It's very hard to negotiate your own job offer. It really is. The most difficult way to do this is verbally and in person.

The way to increase your odds for greatest success is to get the written job offer, review it, and then respond in writing. It also happens to be good business etiquette.

What is this etiquette? Well, it's just etiquette, or polite practice, that if you get something in writing, you can respond to it in writing. But taking it a step further, the good business practices culture in some companies is that you can't even call a meeting without an advance written agenda distributed to all participants. In this way, each person can be prepared in advance, and meeting time is spent effectively and efficiently.

By taking the time to thoughtfully go through the written job offer and respond in writing, you are demonstrating your understanding of this kind of "executive functioning." It sends a message to the hiring manager that you appreciate the importance of everyone's time.

If you're going to get someone on the phone and take him or her away from work, you will have prepared that person in advance on where to focus his or her attention so he or she knows what it is you're going to be discussing. You "get it" – you *are one of them*. This makes you look good and sells well.

Not only do we need to care about making you look good (always), but we want to take care to make the hiring manager look good. Or at least avoid making him look bad. It is possible that a problem with authority could hinder your negotiation process.

Now, I'm not talking about you having a problem with authority; I'm talking about the person on the other side of the table having this issue. Some people in Corporate America don't want you to know they don't have authority to make decisions or give you what you are asking for in your negotiations. It would be very embarrassing to them for you to realize they are not as powerful as they want to seem.

So if you surprise such a hiring manager (and, since you don't know which hiring managers fall into this category, we have to assume everyone does) by verbally asking for something on the phone or in person, and he doesn't have the authority to give it to you, it could be too embarrassing for him to tell you, "I have to ask somebody else." If you put someone into a corner like that, often the only answer he feels he can give you is, "No, sorry, we can't do this."

What's your work-around? Put the request in writing. Then when the hiring manager gets it, he has plenty of time to run the request up the chain-of-command, and when you do call him, he will be prepared with an answer—coming directly from him. Hopefully, it's a positive one.

We want the hiring manager to be the one bestowing the request upon you – making him appear all the more powerful. He's happy, you're happy, the relationship starts out happy, so it's all good.

Reactions vs. Responses

One of my clients once told me, "Once I hear the hiring manager's voice on the phone, I lose all objectivity, and it gets really hard for me to talk, let alone to negotiate." Yes, the voice can be a real deal-killer.

Somehow, you don't want to disappoint this person for whom you are going to work, and with whom you are entering this long-term relationship.

So don't set yourself up for disappointment. Let a written initial response do the "heavy lifting" of carrying back your negotiation requests.

Have you ever experienced a scenario like this? The hiring manager says, "Look the job offer over, then give me a call on Tuesday afternoon with any questions."

You have all your negotiation points lined up and dutifully call on Tuesday afternoon. Little do you know that on Tuesday morning, the hiring manager's boss yelled at him because he didn't hit his sales numbers. Then his secretary announced that she's going on maternity leave again for the second time in two years. As if that wasn't enough disruption for one day, his 16-year-old son just had another fender-bender, his third in three months, making his insurance rates soar through the roof.

It is with this backdrop that you, unknowingly, make your phone call to the hiring manager. Your audience is in a very bad mood right now. Wait until you hear the tone of voice that greets you when he picks up that phone. You will have done nothing wrong. You will not be asking for anything unreasonable. But you're still going to experience some fallout from the hiring manager's bad day just because he is a human being, and that's the way things work.

Successful negotiators know that the workaround for this is to **control the timing and delivery of your message**—and to not set yourself up for such a possibility in the first place.

In our scenario above, you are likely to sense a lot of tension from the hiring manager's voice. You will instinctively know this is not a good time to negotiate, but you're stuck on the phone, one-on-one with your new boss. If he says, "Do you have any questions on the offer," you are likely to panic and say, "No, it looks good," and just accept.

If you had written out your response to the offer letter and sent it to the hiring manager, let's say it arrived even on this awfully bad day he was having. After all these things have happened, at the end of his long day, he now reads the printout of your email negotiation requests that his secretary has thoughtfully left for him, and sees how nicely you have asked for an extra $5,000.00 in base pay and two extra weeks of vacation, with a start date a week later than expected.

Due to the frustration of this day, he picks up the printout of your email, and he swears and he throws it in the corner. Fortunately, you are not there to see – or hear – this reaction. It is just a great way for the hiring manager to release the frustration that everything else that happened today has caused.

Fine, we say. Because after the hiring manager gets that out of his system, he will no doubt pick up that printout of the email from you and say to himself, "I feel better now that I released some steam, and I'm going to feel even better once I get this guy on board to help me hit my numbers and start making my life easier. Now what is he asking…?"

Cooler heads will prevail, and a deal will get done. **With our written response, we gave the hiring manager time to react, and then respond to us**. If you just make the phone call, you only give him time to react to you. **Responses are almost always preferable to reactions.**

Timing is very important to negotiations. The scenario described above gives our hiring manager the opportunity to hear what we are saying and process our requests at a time when it is good *for him*. And when the timing is good for him, it's good for us.

We have to understand that there are superseding, intervening forces at play in people's lives that cause bad things to upset their days. These things are not our fault – so don't give them the opportunity to ruin your negotiations.

Is there any downside to putting something in writing? Yes, there is. There's a downside to putting something in writing if you don't do it artfully. Once something is in writing, it can take on a life of its own. Proof. It can be printed out, saved and used against you. Ask any lawyer.

But you're not going to slap just anything down into an email and hit "send." The process in my book is one of proactive negotiation. It requires thoughtful analysis and careful selection of just the right words, and then editing and re-editing every response before anything is finalized and sent.

We are crafting thoughtful responses, never reacting in the immediate moment. **The goal is that when people print out *your* negotiation communications, you will be proud of how those communications represent you, and what they say about your executive potential.**

Whisper Down The Lane

Successful negotiators know that you need to **Control Your Message.**

As you communicate with recruiters, human resources, and the hiring manager about your job offer, and as information travels up the corporate ladder, what you allegedly said can be altered by word of mouth, much like the children's game, "whisper down the lane."

For example, when you speak with your recruiter, HR, or other individuals within the company, your very carefully chosen words come out just a little bit differently each time they are passed from person to person. Sometimes this can result in you allegedly asking for things in a way that sounds less than flattering—or that is just not accurate.

I don't think anyone deliberately means to be harmful. I don't think people try to screw things up. For the most part, people are just trying to help. But we don't have a window for error, and we aren't dealing with intentions; we are dealing with deals – deals that we want to make happen.

You speak your very carefully chosen words to your recruiter. These words go into his ears, through his brain, and invariably, despite how carefully chosen your words are, they're going to come out of the recruiter's mouth just a little bit differently.

Then the human resources person hears the recruiter's words, processes them through her brain, and they come out her mouth to the hiring manager – and her words are just a little different from the recruiter's. So now your message is even more "altered" than your original, very carefully chosen words. This is the way of verbal communications. No one is necessarily trying to misquote you, but it's just how it goes.

I have seen careers derailed in Corporate America due to "miscommunications" such as these. However, there is an extremely simple solution to this problem: convey your carefully crafted message in writing so that there can be no question about what you said or what you want.

Sample Response to a Recruiter

If you're working with a recruiter, and you've received a job offer which is now ready to be negotiated with the hiring manager, I recommend you tell the recruiter something like this:

You:
"Thank you so much for getting us to this point, Mr. Recruiter. You have now taken me to where I can close the final terms of this deal with my hiring manager, and I plan to use this negotiation opportunity as a way to build rapport with my new boss by communicating with him directly from this point forward."

Recruiter:
"I'm not so sure that's a good idea. Compensation discussions can be very sensitive conversations. All communications with the company really need to go through me. I am invested in getting this deal to yes, and of course, want to see that things get done so that you get this job."

You:

"Thank you. I think you are the world's best recruiter and I will use you for the rest of my life, and I will tell all my friends to do so, too. At the same time, I recognize that you have to work for the company, not for me, and I need to use this opportunity to show my boss the caliber of employee that I truly am. I value your input. I want your input, and if you have suggestions for me on what I am proposing to negotiate, or what you suggest I ask for, I welcome them.

In fact, I'm happy to run my draft response through you first. I will be sending an email with my thoughts to the hiring manager by next Tuesday. I will, of course, copy you on anything I send."

Summary: Create for yourself the written trail of communication so there is no doubt as to your exact words, intentions, and message to management.

So now you know about the basics of employment contracts, as well as some secrets and techniques for controlling your message and avoiding the consequences of counteroffers.

Before we move into the Proactive Negotiation Process and how to convey your requests with just the right words to get what you want, the next chapter will focus on how you prepare for negotiations with finding crucial data needed to formulate a persuasive "ask."

Trust me, I know, no one likes homework, but a little time spent in preparation for these negotiations can turn into big dollars when it comes to your new job offer or contract.

As I've emphasized before, the mere fact that you are negotiating means you are taking a risk. It means you have to take your foot off first base if you are ever going to steal second base. I never, ever advocate for crazy risk. But I do advocate for calculated strategic risk, carried out in the right way, at the right time. Preparation is a necessary part of that.

Chapter 3.
Doing Your Homework Before a Negotiation

Anyone who has ever interviewed for a job realizes that as part of that process, it is inevitable that you will be asked the question, "What are your compensation requirements?" We are all savvy enough to know that we want the company to put out that first salary number.

But just in case you do end up in a situation where you have put a dollar number on the table, you don't want to sell yourself short – nor do you want to price yourself out of the competition. What should you do?

What you don't know, quite simply, can kill your deal. The simple solution is that you must do your homework before engaging in new job offer negotiations. I recommend you do this preparation early in the interview process – even well before the "offer" stage.

Fortunately, due to the internet and the popularity of social networking, it has never been easier for candidates to get good background information on a potential employer and a new job opportunity.

In order to be prepared, you need to do a little research into the areas concerning the prospective open position at the company, the company itself, and the industry in which your company does business. This is called researching industry compensation norms, company compensation norms, and regional compensation norms (because different areas of the country have a higher cost of living than others, and thus pay more).

All of these factors, plus the salary range for the job, will figure into your job offer negotiations. We'll examine each of these factors in more detail.

Salary Range

The first thing you'll probably research is the salary range for the job. This will help give you a good ballpark idea for where the salary should be when management makes the job offer to you.

But salary is only one component of compensation. In order to find the most accurate numbers for all aspects of compensation – base pay, bonuses, stock options or other long term incentives, benefits, perks (like car allowances or other things) – you will want to research industry norms, company norms, and position norms, as mentioned above.

How do people doing the job you are doing typically get paid – generally, in the industry and in this company? What are all the aspects of pay that go into the compensation arrangement? We want to know these details.

Of course, base pay, or salary, is most often the biggest and most important part of any compensation package. "Salary range" means the range of pay that has been established by the company to be paid to employees performing a particular job or function.

A salary range will have a minimum pay rate, a maximum pay rate, and a mid-point, with opportunities for pay increases in between. If you are deemed competent to perform the job, you should be hired in at least at the mid-point range.

Depending on the level of the job, there can be a wide variation between the minimum and the maximum points in a salary range, and the more executive level the job, the wider the salary range tends to be.

Where can you find general salary survey information? The U.S. Bureau of Labor Statistics is a good place to start. *The Occupational Outlook Handbook* includes national and state wage projections as well as data for seven major occupational divisions, which include hundreds of occupations.

A variety of salary range calculator tools are also available online, so you can prepare in advance with some salary range estimates of your own. A few are listed here. Check out these web sites for more information on executive compensation:

- www.Monster.com
- www.TheLadders.com
- www.PayScale.com
- www.Salary.com
- www.Findlaw.com
- www.Rileyguide.com
- www.CareerBuilders.com

You can also subscribe to a variety of executive compensation subscription services, to purchase more specific salary comparison information called "data points." To avoid incurring a subscription expense to these services, see if your attorney can get this information for you when you need it.

For example, if you were interviewing for a job as the Vice President of Marketing for a pharmaceutical company in the dermatological space in the northeast region of the US, with sales of $500 million/year, and with 1,000 employees or fewer, you might want to buy data points for perhaps 5 comparable positions in the same region, in the same therapeutic space, and for companies of the same size. Then you would know that the compensation data (typically base pay, bonus, and stock option information) you received truly was "comparable" to the offer you expect to receive.

Regional Norms

To determine their salary ranges, companies often pay large Human Resources consulting firms, like Hay Group or Towers Watson, to conduct market pay studies for jobs within the organization. They provide HR with data compiled on people doing similar work in similar industries in the same region of the country. From this data, HR determines what the "regional norm" or salary range should be for a particular job.

Companies also consider the cost of living in a particular area of the country when determining a regional salary range. It only makes sense that it will cost more to live in Los Angeles than in Boise. But even if the company forgets this detail, we won't.

The cost of living varies widely across the US, and sometimes taking a job even just one state away can require a 50% increase in salary just to keep you "even."

For example, I have negotiated many agreements for employees relocating from the Philadelphia area to the New York City or northern New Jersey areas – and if you enter the "here" versus "there" zip codes into either the Chamber of Commerce's Cost of Living Index Calculator, or www.HomeFair.com 's cost of living salary calculator, you may be surprised to see that you do need, in many instances, a very significant salary increase just for the employee to maintain his standard of living for such a relocation.

Most employees don't want to relocate just to "stay even" – they want a pay increase, so that has to be factored into any new job negotiations.

Often salary ranges, or the studies and data supporting them, are not freely shared. Don't let that deter you. Just ask.

Salary is not a secret subject now; it's a topic that is on the table. You and the hiring manager are talking about it, so no one needs to feel shy. For heaven's sake, "transparency" is a buzz word in corporate-speak these days, and since the company has paid an awful lot of money to get that salary survey information, why not share it?

Some companies will just come right out and tell you what the range is for a job if you ask. For example, if you are asked, "What are your compensation requirements?" you could respond, "I would expect to be paid commensurate with the responsibilities of this position and with my experience. What is the salary range for this position?"

If the company is not forthcoming, you will at least be prepared, based upon your own research, to offer a number for the job that you feel is merited, based upon your own financial needs, experience, and the research you have done. It is amazing what great results you can achieve when you substantiate your requests with objective, measurable data.

Industry and Company Norms

To keep current with industry compensation norms, or what an industry generally is doing in regards to compensation, read industry publications and contact industry professional associations for recent studies and compensation surveys. This is another good reason to maintain your membership in professional societies.

Industry and individual company research reports can be obtained from commercial sources, a few of which are listed below (none of which I am endorsing or recommending):

- www.ibisworld.com
- www.hoovers.com
- www.ovum.com
- www.dandb.com (Dun & Bradstreet)

You can also search online data libraries, government websites, and web search engines like Google to get more insight into the vast amount of information that is available on the web about companies and industries – and not just about their compensation data. For example, ask questions like this:

- Is the company fiscally sound?
- Is it "in play" for a take-over (meaning your job could be short-lived, and you'd better be negotiating for severance pay)?
- Are any of the company's products involved in significant products liability litigation?
- If the company is privately held, how do shareholders (like you) get a liquidity event if they exit before either a sale of the company or an initial public offering?
- What is the background and character of the executive team, based on past job performance. Did they leave their former companies in good stead, or in a shambles?

Good examples of some resources to check include the following:

- BizJournals.com
- LinkedIn Company Profiles
- The SEC Website (SEC.gov) – for information on publicly-traded companies (http://www.sec.gov/edgar/searchedgar/companysearch.html)
- The Wall Street Executive Library – ExecutiveLibrary.com/Research.asp
- Governance Metrics International

- International Association of Corporate and Professional Recruitment

The U.S. Securities and Exchange Commission's EDGAR database is a particularly useful tool to keep in your arsenal. All publicly-traded U.S. companies are required to report compensation for their top executives and members of their boards of directors to the SEC. This information is compiled into a database called "EDGAR." You can obtain helpful compensation data free from EDGAR.

To get comparative information about any offer you are considering, select a few competitive companies similar in size and industry then go to EDGAR's "Search for Company Filings" and search EDGAR for each company. You can search for the most recent definitive proxy statement – the SEC Form DEF 14A – as it will tell you what was to be voted upon at the annual shareholder meetings (for example, the executive compensation plan). This will lead you to the documents you may want to review. Then scan the filed documents to find anything to do with "compensation".

If this process sounds too difficult for you, often just typing the company's name and search words like "SEC" and "severance plan" or "compensation plan" into your favorite web search engine will get you started with a lot of good information.

Networking

Networking is generally defined as the exchange of information or services among individuals, or the cultivation of productive relationships for employment or business. It's the old-fashioned way of friends asking friends for help. It's still the preferred way of executives for making things happen (like job offers) because it works.

While web research can help you find the data you need to support your negotiations, it is always a good idea to network with real people. It's the personal touch. However, because asking for salary information can be a touchy subject, you have to be careful how you approach people, or with whom you try to make connections to have these conversations. The first place to turn is to long-time, trusted friends and family as the basic building blocks of your network. These friends can be people with whom you attend church or coach soccer. They can be friends with whom you went to school, who belong to your club, or who live in your neighborhood. Anyone is fair game.

Ask these trusted advisors if they know people who could put you into contact with the right individuals within your targeted industry or companies. With a facilitated introduction, you can then make a personal contact and get to know these people.

When you get a one-on-one meeting, I would then ask very general questions about the company, the job, the position, and see what type of specific information the individual may be willing to share with you as rapport builds.

Be aware that exchanges conducted by email or other written mechanism, do leave a "paper trail," and I recommend that be avoided due to the confidentiality risks. You are more likely to get the most honest exchanges – and the most useful information– in a personal, one-on-one meeting, usually over a meal or coffee.

You can cast a wider net for information by extending your in-person networking efforts and joining groups that network and hold events with other executives within your community. For example, you may want to belong to ExecuNet, or if you are in the Philadelphia region, perhaps the Greater Philadelphia Senior Executive Networking Group.

Consider one of the local chapters of national organizations such as the Financial Executives Networking Group, Financial Executives International, American Institute of CPAs, ChemPharma Professional Association, The Professional Women's Roundtable, The Association of Women Entrepreneurs, the Chamber of Commerce (and its Society of Professional Women organization), one of the local Bar Associations (if you are an attorney) – you get the drift.

There are more groups than I could name. Your professional associations are a great place to get a more comprehensive list of groups that may be right for your professional area of work. But I believe in "cross-pollination" – you will get leads from lots of places, not just from those within your area of work, so get out and about, and network. Don't forget your networks within service organizations such as Rotary Clubs, Kiwanis Clubs, and United Way.

Job fairs or expos that are based on your industry can also be good networking venues. At these career placement events, questions about salary and other aspects of the industry are encouraged, and you can use them to collect data, even if you are not particularly interested in any of the employers. These large-scale gatherings can provide a great wealth of knowledge and occur quite often in major cities.

You can also acquire salary information through outplacement firms and career counseling services, if you are fortunate enough to have this service while transitioning between jobs. These firms help guide their clients through the job search process and can provide a wealth of resources.

Web Networking

In my experience, today's executives appreciate that another acceptable way to get information about an open position is to discreetly approach their connections via professional networking sites, like LinkedIn to find a contact within the company and ask questions about the open position.

In that way, candidates can get "the real story" about what the job is like, what the boss is like, what the compensation is likely to be, and what it's like to work for the company. In a social media world, this is the way information travels. Please know: smart executives do not openly post and Twitter these communications to the entire world. These are the kinds of requests that are verbal and are made through people they know, to and though a network, so that this is truly a "discreet" – as in "negotiation secret" – process.

The Other Social Networking Way to Get the "Insider's Perspective"

If you don't have personal contacts within a company with whom you can network, don't despair. Social networking has a fallback position for you: counterculture websites where anyone can post freely about what it is like to work for a particular employer or boss. You can search for what current and former employees have to say about what it's really like to work for your prospective new employer, and you can go into your interview more prepared than ever!

These websites allow people to post information about compensation and working conditions – a few are listed below (caveat: the life span of some websites can be akin to that of a housefly):

- www.GlassDoor.com
- www.Vault.com
- www.Jobeehive.com
- www.Jobitorial.com
- www.Pingmycompany.com
- www.CafePharma.com

Summary of Part I

Now that you've done your homework and have not only a good compensation range in mind for this job, but a virtual intelligence dossier of background information compiled about the company, you are ready to move forward with the actual negotiations.

At this point, you understand how employment contracts work as well as the benefits of getting the positive terms we negotiate into some type of written agreement.

You understand that negotiation has risk, but if we use positive words and other techniques that don't sound like a "counteroffer," the odds are good that we won't lose this deal just because we try to negotiate for some reasonable enhancements to the first job offer.

Your research has shown you how other comparable companies in the region and industry are compensating people doing similar work.

You have networked with people who have actual knowledge about similar jobs in the industry and with those who have actual knowledge of the company extending us the offer. You have also checked the counter-culture web sites to see what ex-employees have said about this company and have factored that information into your decision.

You feel you are ready to convey your requests. You just need to be sure you do so in a way that your prospective new employer can truly "hear your message" and perceive it positively.

Now it is time to apply the basic principles we learned in Part I of this book to the Proactive Negotiation Process that follows in Part II.

❖ ❖ ❖

Part II.
The Proactive Negotiation Process– The Strategy

Chapter 4.
Analyze the Offer

The usual course of business is that the job offer arrives in writing, as an offer letter, or more likely today as an offer email. A million things are running through your mind, not the least of which is, "Just take it!"

Allow yourself to feel all the good feelings of validation and worth that receiving a job offer brings. You've earned it! Gratitude for the offer is merited. And we will surely express that as part of our Proactive Negotiation Process.

What we won't do is let our gratitude cross over the line to groveling and reach the point that stops us from negotiating.

Many studies have been done about the adverse, long-term financial effects that occur by never negotiating job offers or salary. In the book *Women Don't Ask: Negotiation and the Gender Divide*, authors Linda Babcock and Sara Laschever focus on typical negotiating behavior of women. Among their many statistics they indicate that over a woman's career, if she never negotiates her salary, she could lose $1 million over her lifetime.

You might ask yourself, how can this be? Well, in his book *The Salary Tutor*, Jim Hopkinson figured that if you started out at age twenty-one with an annual income of $20,000, received 5% raises annually, and retired at age sixty-five, you would accrue lifetime earnings of $3 million. But, even if you negotiated just a "teeny-tiny bit," and received 6% raises instead of 5% raises, Hopkinson shows that your lifetime earnings would jump to $4 million – an additional $1 million in salary over your lifetime. There's the missing million.

There are a lot of reasons why people "don't ask" – fear, lack of preparation, lack of knowledge, anxiety – you name it. The fact that you are reading this book means that you are beyond that point now.

You are reading this book because you know that negotiation is acceptable; in fact, it is often expected from someone at your level. And you are ready and willing to negotiate.

You are ready to hone your skills and learn what the top executives know so that you can prove to the company that it made the right choice in selecting you from the large pool of available candidates. How can the company tell this? From how you conduct yourself during the negotiation process.

When you negotiate, you are on stage. It is a wonderful opportunity to showcase your talents and abilities, and to validate to the company how right it was in selecting you.

Start seeing the negotiation process in this way, and embrace it as an opportunity to shine because you have "the right stuff," and the company wants to see that you have executive potential for even bigger jobs in the future. The company wants validation ("We were so right to hire this person"!) and we are going to give it to them.

How do you take the first offer from its initial form, and make it the best offer it can possibly be? In order to accomplish this goal, there are a few simple, yet extremely important steps you must take.

This chapter, and the ones that follow in Part II of this book, will outline the steps I recommend as part of the Proactive Negotiation Process for making your job offer the best it can be.

To help you visualize and remember how this Proactive Negotiation Process is different from other methods, I have given it the name "It's AWL About the Law."

No, I'm not referring to the small, pointed tool called the awl (used for a variety of creative needs from carpentry to sail making to shoe repairs to bookbinding). But in fact, when we negotiate, we are sharp, and our responses are pointed, so there is some analogy.

The name AWL for my purposes is an acronym formed from the initials of the key words from the steps in my Proactive Negotiation Process. The chapters that follow will go through the "It's AWL About the Law" process in detail for you.

Here's the basic 4-step Proactive Negotiation Process that the AWL acronym will help you remember: Analyze the new job offer, then develop your wish list. Next, WIIFM your wish list and then convey those items to your hiring manager with a love letter.

This sounds simple, and not very legalistic – which is exactly why it is successful for the job offer negotiation process! But once you delve into the details that follow, you'll see that it's not as simple as it sounds, and that to be truly successful, every word and nuance can make a big difference in the outcome you achieve.

Remember, our goal is to massage the message and then negotiate in a positive way that leaves our hiring manager feeling good about us and the experience of negotiating with us. Then once the deal is in place, it is all (or "AWL") binding under the law.

Step 1: Analysis

The first step in my Proactive Negotiation Process is making an analysis of the offer you have been given by your future employer. "Analyze" means to examine something methodically and in detail in order to understand all of its parts. **The "A" in AWL is for Analysis.**

Your analysis will focus on:
1.   What is **good** in the offer letter.
2.   What is **bad** in the offer letter.
3.   What is **missing** from the offer letter.

It is hard to know what should or should not be in your offer letter or agreement since each client has different needs and will want different things.

If you go to www.jobsecretagent.com, I post a checklist of sample clauses that are typically found in employment contracts. I keep the information on the web site so it can be updated as needed. You can use this checklist as a guideline of topics you may want to put on your "analysis" list of things you'd like to have – or not have – in your agreement with your new employer.

During your analysis, you will look over the terms in the company's proposed offer letter or agreement, applying your knowledge of contracts and their components from Chapter 1 of this book.

As you carefully read the document, pay specific attention to the terms it contains. Which terms are good for you? Which ones need some tweaking to be good for you? Which ones need to go? Which ones are totally missing from the document?

Of course, any offer or agreement will contain "the basics" we discussed in Part I- information such as your base pay, the start date, the person to whom you report, and the location of your work. Sometimes these are fine as is; sometimes even these need work.

Salary is a prime example of a term to be negotiated: most of the time, clients would like base pay to be enhanced, or at least made to be "no less than" a certain number each year. Put that on your list.

Often times, we can use the start date—when you will begin working at your new job—as a bargaining chip – something to "give" in on, in exchange for something else for which we are asking.

Stating the primary location of work can be critically important if we add a termination by executive "for Good Reason" clause; if the company then moves that location of work beyond any agreed-upon mile radius at some future date, it will trigger your right to collect severance pay.

In my experience, you will find that often times, it's what is missing from the offer letter or agreement that turns out to be the most important. Examples most frequently include severance pay, particulars of equity, commission details, change of control clauses, bonus guarantees, creative incentive compensation arrangements, work-from-home arrangements, relocation perks, etc.

Every person is different and will benefit differently from unique tweaks to the terms in his or her job offer or agreement. If you do not see something in your offer that you wanted to obtain, or that you believe is important to you, it is essential that you raise the matter as part of the analysis process. Details that may seem tedious and small can lead to major headaches later on if not handled correctly in the contract negotiation process.

By learning how to organize and present terms in a way that gives you a fighting chance in your negotiations, you give yourself a solid shot at having them inked into writing in your final employment deal. Often some of the most key terms within any executive's new job offer are those about the equity, or long-term incentive, component.

Knowing how to analyze this aspect of executive compensation is so important that I am devoting the next chapter to it as part of negotiating a job offer.

Chapter 5.

How to Compare Long-Term Incentives and Equity

Meaningful Comparisons of Long-Term Incentives

If you are considering a new job offer, before you can truly evaluate how good it is, you need to do an apples-to-apples comparison of that competing offer against the total value of the compensation and benefits you already enjoy with your current employer.

If your current compensation package consists of only base pay, medical benefits, and an annual bonus, then the comparison will be easy to do. However, companies today are offering a wide variety of elements in their compensation plans, and all of them need to be considered in your analysis of how sweet a deal this new job offer truly is.

Whereas your annual bonus is a measure of your short-term performance, many companies are also using long-term incentive plans as a part of their overall compensation strategies to accomplish a variety of additional goals over a longer time line.

Long-term incentive programs are designed to reward employees that influence the company's growth. Employees whose jobs are deemed to influence the company's overall long-term performance in key ways are often incentivized to perform by being given a financial stake in the company. In other words, their compensation is structured so that it will fluctuate – up or down – depending upon the company's performance results over time.

There are several types of long-term incentives. In addition to the base pay and annual bonus components to your compensation package, you could see an offer that includes any combination of long-term incentives like the following: stock options, restricted stock units ("RSUs"), phantom stock, performance units or performance shares, warrants, or stock appreciation rights.

Long-term compensation links an employee's financial rewards to his or her contributions to the company's performance beyond the one-year point. These long-term incentives generally include the following 3 goals: (1) encourage employees to stay employed with the company, (2) accomplish long-term performance goals, and (3) link the payment of long-term financial rewards to the individual's and/or the company's achievement of long-term business plan successes that drive shareholder value.

The issues surrounding long-term incentives can be complex. Different types of long-term incentives have different vesting schedules, and there are forfeiture issues if you leave employment prior to vesting dates. Each type of benefit can have different tax implications. Some require you to make an initial investment, and others do not. And then, of course, you have to try to estimate or calculate the value of these often complicated perks.

To fully address all the types of long-term incentive compensation and equity, and the detailed issues that can arise in compensation agreements related to long-term incentive compensation and equity, would be beyond the scope of this book. And I'm betting you don't have the time or inclination to become an executive compensation expert anyway, so let's limit our focus to some key practical applications for job offer negotiations that you can add to your toolkit.

If you are a senior-level employee, you will likely hire someone like me to review your deal paperwork, and help make sure you don't lose ground when making a decision as important as a new job offer. Honestly, I believe that if you are being offered stock options, long-term incentives or equity in any form, you should invest in having an attorney who is well-versed in executive compensation and employment matters review those documents for you before you sign them. Your decision in this matter could mean the difference between hundreds of thousands of dollars that you do – or do not – realize.

There are some steps you can take on your own to better determine the true value of each job offer you are considering so you can make a more valid comparison between a job offer – and a "killer" job offer.

Let's try to hit some of the highlights so you can know what information you need to make a more intelligent decision and job offer comparison, and then you can do additional research on your own.

Here are the 5 key areas to analyze about long-term incentives so you can begin your apples-to-apples comparison, and the creation of your "killer" job offer:

1.   Is the offer from a publicly-traded or a privately-held company?
2.   What is the form of long-term incentive being offered?
3.   Is there a mix of long-term incentive vehicles?
4.   What are the details of all the vesting schedules?
5.   What does company performance tell me?

Publicly-traded vs. Privately-held Company Equity Offerings

Equity represents some form of ownership in the company. That ownership is reflected in shares. Shares can be restricted or limited by the type issued, and any such restrictions need to be explored so that you can determine the value of the equity you are receiving. For example, will your shares have voting rights? Are there preferential shares, and if so, in what order will your shares be paid in the event the company is sold? Do your shares have participation rights to the profits at the time the company is sold?

Subject to possible restrictions, equity in publicly-traded companies has a ready market of prospective buyers – the public, able to buy stock over exchanges like the New York Stock Exchange, NASDAQ and others. Once your "in the money" shares are vested and owned by you, you have a wide range of potential buyers to whom you can freely sell them.

There is no ready market for equity of privately-held companies; thus, when you leave your employment in such a company, you cannot sell your shares to anyone except as permitted in the Stock Plan or Stock Agreement that you signed.

This can be a huge problem – can you get your money out when you want it, or at all? Will your shares have any value, or be severely discounted in value due to a lack of liquidity, and your lack of ability to control the decisions and direction of the company? If a significant part of your compensation package is in equity, how can you tell if you'll ever be able to cash this out in the event your employment is terminated involuntarily without cause?

You should be getting the message here about how important it is to ask for and read the Stock Plan, as well as any documents (like the stock option award agreement) you will be asked to sign related to equity in a privately-held company. Determine for yourself your best projections of the company's growth potential and future value – figuring in a discount for the lack of control and liquidity (no ready market) – and then develop a negotiating strategy around any problems before you sign on the dotted line. This is an area where your attorney and accountant can be of assistance.

Stock Options and Vesting Schedules

Upon joining the company some employees are given actual shares of stock or "stock grants" as a signing bonus, but most employees are not given shares right away; rather, they get equity in a form that has to be held over time, or vest, before it actually becomes something the employee owns. A vesting date is the date on which you have the right to receive a promised benefit.

A "stock option" is a form of equity that vests over time. It gives you the right to purchase a specific number of shares of stock in the future at a fixed price (the exercise price) and for a fixed period of time. These specifics are outlined in a written stock option award document. Even though the market price of a publicly-traded stock will fluctuate over time, your exercise price is fixed in your award document.

How much value you receive from your options depends on the future price of the stock when the options reach their vesting dates. If the company grows and performs well, then most likely the market price in the future will exceed your exercise price, and your options will be "in the money" – meaning you have gain.

Your gain, if you choose to exercise the options, is the difference between the stock's market price at the time of exercise, and the exercise price of your stock option award agreement. You have likely realized a lot more compensation than you originally expected when you signed the stock option award agreement.

But what if the company does not grow or perform well over time? Well, when those options vest, the stock price at market value will be below the exercise price stated on your stock option award agreement. This means the options are "under water" and have no value.

You can hold on to them for the life of the option grant (usually 10 years) and hope they recover in value so that you can get some gain. If the value of the stock does not increase, there is no obligation to exercise the options. If the options do not recover in value before the life of the option, then the option expires – and you have failed to realize the compensation you expected.

Stock options encourage the employee to perform well and to remain employed with the company, knowing that as time passes, that equity will mature and become theirs. Employers like options and other benefits that vest over time, as programs like these encourage – and reward – employee achievement, retention, loyalty, and commitment to the company's goals and mission.

A typical stock option vesting schedule is likely to be three or four years, vesting in equal pro-rata (one-third or one-fourth) portions on each anniversary date of the grant.

For example, on your start date of April 15, 2013, you are granted 10,000 stock options, vesting in equal shares over the next four years. If your offer says you will start vesting right away, then on April 15 for each of the next four years, you will vest ownership in one-fourth, or 2,500, of the options, until on April 15, 2017, all 10,000 of the options will be vested and "owned" by you.

You can now decide if, based upon the company's stock price, they have value, and if you want to exercise the options and get shares of stock in exchange. Your offer letter may, however, set forth a requirement that you have a "waiting year" before your options start vesting. If that is the case, then the vesting schedule will be one year later than in my example – pushing out your realization date to April 15, 2018.

If you are evaluating a job offer, having a waiting year before vesting begins is not something you want to see, as it pushes out the time horizon for achievement of this important component of your compensation. And what if your employment is terminated before each vesting date? Well, unless you can negotiate otherwise, you will likely lose the value of all options that were not yet vested as of your employment termination date.

Here's a possible work-around: Try negotiating for 25% of the equity vesting on the one-year anniversary of your start date, with the balance to vest 1/36th each month thereafter that you work. In this way, you very quickly get to ownership of smaller pieces of the pie – but ownership is the key objective, and faster is usually better for the employee.

Clearly, when comparing offers, you need to look at vesting schedules of the relative offers to see which is more favorable to getting you to ownership more quickly. Then ask yourself how likely it is that you will remain with the company long enough to realize the value of this benefit.

Statistically speaking, the longer the vesting horizon, the less likely it is that any employee will get to the pot of gold at the end of the rainbow. In assigning a value in your comparison, give a lesser, or discounted, value to the benefits you expect to receive during any later vesting years due to the uncertainty of your realizing these benefits.

Options and Restricted Stock Units

Whereas most companies historically used stock options as the preferred long-term incentive for employees, with new accounting rules, it has become unfavorable for companies to carry stock options as an expense on their books.

Therefore, many long-term incentive compensation programs have moved away from using only stock options toward a combination of stock options with other vehicles, like restricted stock units, as a form of "golden handcuffs" – a way to reward performance so well that employees are discouraged from leaving the company.

A restricted stock unit is an outright grant of shares in the company, to which the employee does not have immediate access rights. The grant comes with restrictions that lapse with the passage of time.

Typically, RSUs are granted like options – in tranches that vest a portion at a time over a longer period of time. But here's the big difference: whereas a stock option gives the employee the right to purchase shares of stock at some future time if the stock's market price rises above the exercise price, the RSU gives the employee the right to receive the shares in the future without any payment – and the RSU has value regardless of what the stock's future market price may be. This can make a very big difference to the employee's bank account.

For example, if the company grants you 1,000 RSUs when the stock price is $25.00, your units have a potential value of $25,000.00 at the date of the grant. When the vesting date is achieved, the market price of the company's stock may be above or below the price it was on the date of the grant.

If the market price is $35.00/share on the vesting date of your RSUs – great news, your units are now worth $35,000.00, and that is what you are paid, less taxes of course. Conversely, if hard times befall the company, and on the vesting date of your RSUs, the company's stock price has fallen to $15.00/share – still good news: your units are not "under water" (without value) like your stock options are. Your RSUs have a diminished pre-tax value of $15,000.00 – but this still represents value that you can take to the bank.

As in our previous example about stock options under the section on "Vesting Schedules," your offer may state that one-third of the RSUs will vest each year over a three year period. However, just as with options, there are other ways RSUs can vest (like all at once at the end of the appointed vesting period, or smaller percentages vest in the first few years with a larger percentage vesting in the final year), so you have to read what your offer letter says about this. Read any RSU agreement you may be asked to sign, and at least have a general idea of what questions to ask.

I tell clients to visualize RSUs like this: the employer has placed valuable shares into a safe deposit box which has a time lock on it. When the appointed time arrives, the lock will magically open, and the shares inside will be theirs. If the employee's employment is terminated prior to that magic moment, the rule generally is that all unvested restricted units are going to revert back to the company – but this is subject to the terms of the plan document, and your negotiation skills.

Again, you'll need to assess how likely it is that you will remain with the company long enough to realize the value of this benefit and figure that into your comparison calculations.

How to Compare Equity Offerings

If you have stock options with your current employer, look at your statement, or participant summary report, to find the value. The exercise price is the price at which the option was issued to you. This price will never change over the life of your option, even though the market price will change frequently.

If the stock is publicly-traded, check the price at which it is currently trading on the market, and the difference between that price and the exercise price is your value.

Since it is quite common for companies to issue senior level employees options or RSUs each year, you will have to do a value analysis of *each year's* vested options. Of course, as we discussed above, only options that have vested are owned by you and have truly measurable value. You'll have to estimate the value of the unvested options – and I always do that, and figure it into any negotiation equation.

Plan to develop a strategy to negotiate for the value of the unvested options, either with the new employer, or as you are leaving your current employer, depending on all the circumstances of your situation.

As stated before, all options have a defined life – usually ten years from vesting. If you don't exercise the options within their stated lifetime, they will expire and you cannot exercise them. That could be like walking away from money lying on the table!

If your options are with a privately-held company, determining value is not as easy. Usually the company's board of directors or ownership sets a share price based on a business valuation or upon some factor of EBITDA.

EBITDA, or "earnings before interest, taxes, depreciation, and amortization," is one way that most people can legitimately guesstimate the value of a business without paying for a costly private valuation of the company by an appraiser. I'm not a CPA, but generally will tell you that EBITDA is calculated by subtracting expenses from revenue (excluding interests and taxes) without depreciation and amortization (what you pay for tangible and intangible assets).

If the privately-held company won't share financials with you, offer to sign a confidentiality and non-disclosure agreement as an inducement to get them to release the information. If that won't work, have your attorney try to work directly with the company's attorney. If that is not successful, I recommend you do your own independent research, and make your best judgment about the potential for growth, the security and mix of customers, and other factors relative to a company's value and strength that would affect your valuation of its equity interests.

Remember, it's growth potential that drives the future value of most equity awards and incentives. You have to make your best determination of that factor before deciding to tie your future fortunes to those of a prospective new employer.

Keep in mind my caution that any minority ownership interest in a privately-held company is generally discounted for lack of liquidity and control. You need to seriously scrutinize the documentation to determine the likelihood that you will be able to get paid the value of your equity upon any termination of your employment.

Look at Company Performance

Publicly-held companies are required to file a comprehensive summary of their annual performance with the Securities and Exchange Commission. This filing is called a Form 10-K. Most companies disclose on their Forms 10-K whether the companies make their periodic and current reports available for free on their websites, so if the information is there, go get it.

If you can't get the information you need on a company's web site, then look for that company's Form 10-K, and other SEC filings on the SEC's EDGAR database at http://www.sec.gov/edgar.shtml.

The other SEC filings I referenced above include quarterly company financial reports called Form 10-Qs.

If the company experiences a significant event, like the departure of a key executive or a bankruptcy, then the company has to file a Form 8-K to provide a public information update.

Any of these types of SEC forms can provide you with good financial and other information you may need in assessing company performance.

For privately-held businesses, it is more difficult to obtain truly comparative performance data and industry benchmarks. These entities are often not held to the same accounting and transparency standards required of publicly-traded companies.

Often privately-held businesses involve majority ownership by family members or founders. This type of ownership can bring into play issues you will need to explore regarding matters of capital, succession, control, business savvy, and if there is the requisite expertise to take the business to the next level and keep it a viable competitor.

I've had clients go to privately-held companies who thought for sure they wanted my client to be a "change agent" – only to learn that the last thing the companies really wanted was change. You need to be prepared that this could happen to you, and negotiate for terms that protect you from this eventuality.

Let's examine some sample questions you can ask yourself as you look at company performance. If you have offers from competing companies, how do the companies stack up against each other and the other competitors within their industry?

To get some answers, you can look at sales strength, product viability, and profits announced. Is one a stronger market player than the other? Does one own a niche that is likely to grow over time? Each of these questions requires thoughtful analysis before any one statistic becomes meaningful.

Here are some other questions I recommend you ask:

- Do you perceive a company that is truly growing organically, versus by acquisition, as fiscally stronger, and thus more attractive?
- What do you know about the strength and character of the management teams?
- Where do you think you'll have a better fit?
- Which company is on top of the technology curve?
- Which company do you think has the best chance of being in business ten or twenty years from now?

The sky is the limit on these questions. To get to the heart of the secrets behind the numbers in the financial statements, research your companies carefully and secure financial reports. See where each has strengths in the areas that matter the most *to you*.

Valuing Your Offer

Some of my clients are more numerically oriented than others. I've synthesized from the approach of those number-crunchers to give you some tips on how you, too, can approach your next job offer analysis in a more value-oriented manner.

I find it helpful when clients prepare a spreadsheet of each component of their current compensation, as well as their new job offer, and then place the actual, or their estimated, value next to each item for which we will negotiate. This helps me, and them, to visualize the deal, and puts comparative numbers on each of the deal's component parts.

For example, write down your current annual salary, your current estimated annual bonus, how much your health benefits are worth, your life insurance, disability benefits, 401K match, vacation time, car allowance, etc. Then put a dollar value on each item.

Now do the same thing for each component of the new job offer. (You can do the spreadsheet to compare between two job offers, and of course, can take out the column for a current employer if you are not employed.)

Don't forget to factor in the cost-of-living if relocation is required for the new job. For example, if you have to relocate to high cost areas like southern California or east coast cities (New York, northern New Jersey, Washington D.C., Philadelphia, etc.), and you currently live in Las Vegas, or Florida, your cost of housing can increase very significantly.

Next, work in the estimated values of the long-term incentives and more complicated perks that we just discussed like stock options and restricted stock units. I know it can be difficult to put an exact value on these items, and that your values may just be guess-timates, but that is OK – it is your best estimate of comparing apples-to-apples, and sometimes that is all you can do.

Those of you who are trying to do this yourself and who are proficient with Excel can use the Excel net present value function to generate a net present value number for your future after tax cash flow, as some of my clients have done.

As we discussed above, if you think it is less likely you will receive some benefits of one job versus the other (for example, getting RSUs is more risky due to a longer vesting time line, and thus it is theo-retically less likely to happen when compared to the benefits offered in another job offer), use a higher discount rate when valuing the benefits for the risk-ier position.

Do this for each of your offers and then compare your resulting numbers. You now have a useful tool to use in helping you make a knowledgeable decision about the job offer. And together we know where we need to focus our attention in the next steps in our job offer negotiations.

Chapter 6.
Create Your Wish List

To recap, step one in The Proactive Negotiation Process "It's AWL About the Law" is to **A**nalyze the job offer, identifying what is good, what is not so good, and what is missing.

Step two is now to take that analysis and from it create your "**W**ish list," identifying all of the topics you want to address in your negotiations.

The "W" in AWL stands for "Wish List." From this list, we will prioritize how we are going to tackle each topic in our communications back to the hiring manager.

When I work with clients in helping them to create their wish lists, I'll frame it this way: "We have an offer that's on the table. Now if I could turn this into the perfect job for you, what would it look like?

For example, is the base pay in the right *range* -- and if it is, how far can we push it to be *just right*? What should your incentive compensation look like?

How about your severance package? Who would you report to? When would you be eligible for a raise?"

I tell my clients that in a negotiation, there can be so many different things to consider that to keep track of them all, we need to write a list of what we want to achieve. This is what I call a "wish list."

Step 2: Create Your Wish List – What Would Make This The Perfect Job for You?

For example, your Step One analysis of the offer has revealed that there are a few clauses or terms that you would like to have included in your contract. However, there are also a few things about which you are unsure, you have questions, or you would like to have removed from your contract.

All of these topics will end up on your "wish list" in one way or another. Here is just one sample wish list:

Sample Wish List:
1. Base pay $10,000 - $15,000 higher
2. Severance protection to be added
3. Three weeks of vacation vs. two
4. Can I be considered for promotion to next grade level after year one?
5. Is there a non-compete clause hidden in the "Confidentiality" agreement referenced in the offer letter?

6. Specify in the agreement to whom I report and level of my position

7. Is there a work from home policy and do I qualify?

8. Where is my primary place of work, and if that changes, do I have to move? If I don't want to move, I want to be eligible to receive severance pay.

9. We'd like to be able to use the relocation package for up to 18 months, and not sell the house right away due to _____ (children in school, home being under water, spouse's job, etc.)

10. My spouse will have to quit a six-figure job as part of the relocation. We'd like him/her to have career counseling services as part of the relocation package.

I have had clients with 20 topics on a wish list, and those with 2-3 topics on a wish list. The "wish list" is just that – a wish list. This doesn't mean we are going to end up asking for all 20 things. But this is your time to take that offer and attempt to make it as perfect for you as possible.

Now is when you think about everything, the whole big picture of your future at this company. How would you like it to play out? Don't be afraid to THINK BIG. Maybe I should spell that "Pig"....

Of Pigs and Hogs

The Wish List is a tool. The key to negotiating using this tool is balance. When asking for the items on your wish list, you want to become what I like to call, the "little pig that gets fat," not the "hog that tries to get so fat that it actually gets slaughtered."

But how do you create this balance? How could you possibly convince your new company that the items on your wish list are not you being greedy, but that somehow giving them to you could actually be in the best interest of your new company?

What leverage could you possibly have at a new company in order to convince management that you deserve to have all the items on the wish list materialize in the offer letter or agreement for your dream job? Don't worry. I have an answer, because there is a solution. And that's in the next step of "It's AWL About the Law."

Give Aways

In the course of developing your Wish List, make a column along one side and title it "Give Aways." **In addition to thinking about what you want the company to give you, you need to reflect on what you are willing to give the company as consideration for your requests.**

This shows that you are willing to "give" a little in the negotiations and that you don't just expect to "get".

Give Aways will be different in each deal. Examples include things as simple as conceding to an earlier start date, or to some other term of the deal that is less than ideal, but in the overall scheme of things, doesn't really matter that much to you. I have even given away points that weren't technically on the table.

For example, if you were used to having a car allowance, and were considering accepting a new position where a car allowance was not offered to anyone, surely this would adversely affect the value of your overall compensation package. As part of your salary negotiations, one strategy would be to use the concept of a car allowance as a Give Away -- concede that you will agree to give up a car allowance, and leverage it into a request for additional salary. The negotiation might sound something like this:

"I am willing to concede that I will not receive a car allowance as part of this new position. In past comparable positions, I have received car allowances averaging $400/month and that has been a significant part of my overall compensation package. Without asking you to change any policy, I would like to work with the company to try to minimize this financial setback by working out only a modest 5% increase to my starting base salary. This would still put me within the pay range for the position, and

is reasonable for an employee with my skill level and years of experience who can hit the ground running and start delivering results right away for you."

Some readers may say, "But they never offered you a car allowance in the first place." That may be true, but if it's an integral part of the compensation package you are used to having, it is legitimate to make this point. And, if you go back to Chapter 3 on "Doing Your Homework," perhaps we can find justification that it is industry standard for positions in a business like this to have some type of car allowance.

You won't necessarily have a Give Away in every deal, but I recommend you try to find at least one. Then when we convey our requests back to the company, we can lead with a Give Away – making our subsequent requests seem even more reasonable.

Chapter 7.
WIIFM Factors: "What's in it for Me"

Step 3: "WIIFM" Your Way To Negotiating Success

Remember that you have your greatest leverage for negotiations to get things on your wish list now – before you begin working at the new job. Once you are hired (or heaven forbid, begin working without a contract), you are just like every other employee with a badge and ID number, and you will not likely have another opportunity for major deal negotiations until another promotion or new job opportunity arises.

While you are still in the new job offer negotiation process, you are in the best position to take advantage of the fact that the company wants you right now to fill a need that it has, and therefore it is in negotiation mode. This is why the starting pay you negotiate for your new job is so important for your career – and ultimate long-term earnings future.

The essence of business is deal-making, and as many people know, success at deal-making depends on how well you negotiate. Many people have been conditioned to fear the process of negotiating. They are terrified of losing the deal or being rejected. What happens? They lower their goals and sell themselves short.

You've gone this far – I don't want to see you stop here. And believe me, this can be a scary time. You have the offer in hand. You now see a long wish list of things you'd like to negotiate, and all you can think of is, "How do I do this without losing the offer I already have?"

WIIFM – When "Me" Has Nothing To Do With "You"

The most effective way to get the other side to negotiate with you – and to agree with what you are saying – is to spin each request we have on our wish list with a "WIIFM" factor.

In Step 3 of my proactive negotiation process, when I say "WIIFM your way to negotiating success" I mean WIIFM each item on your Wish List to convince the hiring manager why he should give it to you. The "W" in AWL is now doing double-duty: it stands for the two concepts of "WIIFM your Wish List."

WIIFM means "What's In It For Me." AND: this is critical – the "Me" in WIIFM has nothing to do with you! The "Me" refers to the person on the opposite side of the negotiating table.

So when I say we are going to spin our requests with WIIFMs that means that anything we request has to **show the hiring manager what benefits are in it for him and the company if they give us what we are asking.** I strive to answer these basic questions in any WIIFM factor:

- How does what my client is asking create value for the company?
- How does what my client is asking help the company deliver on its goals more effectively or efficiently?
- How does what my client is asking help make the boss look good?

It is basic human nature to respond favorably to things that are to our own advantage. The art of negotiating to "yes" is in choosing just the right way to frame the request and in selecting the strategy and tactics for doing so.

A simple rule of thumb for negotiations is that my client and I must be able to develop a persuasive WIIFM factor for each and every item on our wish list before we ask for that item in our negotiations.

So, this is where the hard work begins. It's very easy to come up with what you'd like to have, and what would make your employment perfect. If you just ask for something because it would make your life easier, or you had it at your last job, that doesn't persuade anyone because you are only thinking about yourself. The hard part is coming up with a way to justify it to your company and your superiors.

In crafting our WIIFMs, we can and do rely on some of the homework we did in Chapter 3 of this book. It is very helpful to turn to the objective, measurable compensation and other data our research uncovered from salary surveys, professional association data, online databases, and the other networking sources referenced in Chapter 3. We can now draw upon these viable resources for our job offer negotiations.

To the extent each and every "ask" of ours is formulated in objective, measurable terms, I believe it strengthens our chances for success. This is based upon 30 years of negotiation experience, and seeing how this approach has worked in practice for thousands of clients. It is also based upon the fact that many people in Corporate America respond well to numbers that support logically presented proposals.

Think about it this way — bosses have a tough life too. Other people are holding them accountable constantly; that's their job. They want to know that you are behind them, that you've got their back, and that you're being supportive of their efforts and achievement of their goals.

This is the way that you have to look at everything – from the perspective of your audience, and not yourself. To illustrate how this can be done, let's look at an example of a common situation: an employee who would like to obtain some extra vacation time.

Example: Create a WIIFM Factor for Two Extra Weeks of Vacation

For example, let's say you come into your negotiations and say to the hiring manager:

"I'd like to have another week of vacation. Actually, I'm used to having two extra weeks, but I'm willing to settle for only one more. That seems fair because everyone at my level had at least this amount of vacation at my last job, and I've been working for 20 years, so I believe that this is a fair amount of vacation to have here too."

Well, truthfully, that "ask" isn't likely to persuade anyone and leave them with a good feeling about you. The boss is likely to be thinking, "I thought you really wanted this job – and all you can think about is how much vacation time you get??"

Statements like the ones above can make you seem more focused on not working than on working. You somehow need to show that you do have in mind the best interests of the company, your boss, and the bigger picture.

Remember, part of negotiation is setting the stage for how the entire employment relationship will unfold for you over the duration of your employment. We want to "showcase" your executive potential, your ability to be promoted, and your unselfish "prince among men" attitude, affirming to the company executives how very lucky they are to have landed such a prize worker. Communications such as the one above will not do the trick.

Instead, perhaps we could WIIFM your extra vacation wish list item like this:

> "*Thank you for the offer of 3 weeks of vacation. I'm used to having 5 weeks, and I'd like to explain my position on that. I understand this job is going to require a big commitment of time and energy. I expect to be working very hard, working many long days and weekends. I am committed and up for the challenge, and that's never been a problem for me, as I love what I do.*
>
> *Historically, I've always found that if I can just take a vacation week every quarter to refresh and restore, I'm a far more effective and efficient worker for my boss and for the company.*
>
> *Although I usually don't even take my full complement of vacation time, I somehow find it comforting to know that it's there if I need it. On that note, I would respectfully request that you grant the two extra weeks of vacation starting with my first year, so I can have five total weeks a year. I know I will*

continue to perform at the top of my game in this position, for you and the company."

Now that is a WIIFM. It has little to do with you. It has everything to do with why that extra week of vacation is going to create value for this company and make the boss look good.

A harsh reality in job offer negotiations is that no one wants to hear too much about you, or what you want or need. You lose ground with that. The power is gained by showing others what is "in it" for them – how your requests can work to their benefit. People do want to hear about what you can do for them. It is basic human nature to want to hear about ourselves.

A Spear in the Side

A company is hiring you for at least one main reason: it has what I like to call "a spear in its side." It has a problem and it needs a work-around. The company has searched far and wide to find the person who can solve its problem, and it has determined that you are that person.

The company needs you to remove the spear from its side; that's why you have the job offer. You need to make sure that you, the candidate, reinforce in your WIIFMs that the company is correct, and that in fact, you are the solution to its problems. Our messages must convey how the company's life will be better once you are a part of the team and have removed that pesky spear from its side.

By conveying your negotiation "asks" in a way that addresses what the company needs, and in a way the company can hear what you are saying, you will improve your odds for achieving success in workplace negotiations.

Timing is always of critical importance. When negotiating any type of contract, you have the greatest negotiating leverage going into the deal before you begin the work or accept the job. If you fear the negotiating process, the "lost opportunity costs" of this mindset are ones you may have to live with for many years.

Summary of Part II

Part II outlines the key strategy-setting aspects of my Proactive Negotiation Process which we call, "It's AWL About the Law". The AWL acronym will help you remember this Proactive Negotiation Process: Analyze the new job offer, then develop your wish list. Next, WIIFM your wish list and then convey those items to your hiring manager with a love letter. Let's recap the first three steps of the process that we've discussed thus far:

1. **Step One: Analysis**. In Part II, we address the "A" and "W" aspects of this acronym. "A" stands

for Analysis of the job offer – the first step in my Pro-active Negotiation Process. Your analysis identifies what's good about the initial job offer, what's not so good about it, and what's missing.

Chapter 5 addresses the important and complex world of long-term incentives. Remember that if you are considering a new job offer, before you can truly evaluate how good it is, you need to do an apples-to-apples comparison of that offer against competing offers, and against the total value of the compensation and benefits you already enjoy with your current employer. This chapter explains some common long-term incentives, and shows you ways to do this critical analysis.

2. **Step Two: Wish List**. The "W" in AWL stands for "Wish List." After you have analyzed the job offer, Step Two of my Proactive Negotiation Process is to take that analysis and from it create your "Wish List," identifying all of the topics you want to address in your negotiations.

From this list, you will prioritize how you are going to tackle each topic in your communications back to the hiring manager.

3. **Step 3: WIIFM Your Wish List**. WIIFM means "What's in it for me." But in this book, the "me" in WIIFM isn't about you. In the "It's AWL About the Law" Proactive Negotiation Process, when I use

WIIFM, I mean, "What's in it for the guy on the other side of the table to give you what you are seeking in these negotiations?"

The "W" in "It's AWL About the Law" is now doing double-duty: it stands for the two concepts of "WIIFM your Wish List." So when I say you are going to spin your requests with WIIFMs that means that anything you request from your Wish List has to be supported by a WIIFM factor that shows the hiring manager what benefits are in it for him and the company if they give you what you are asking.

And how, you may ask, am I going to do all this? The short answer: with the "L" in the "It's AWL About the Law" Proactive Negotiation Process.

Now that you have done the key strategy work, you are ready to take action to maximize your chances for making the final terms of the job offer the best ones for you, and to successfully implement the right negotiation tactics that increase your chances of completing the mission and achieving success. This is Step 4 of the 4-Step AWL Process: convey those items on your wish list to your hiring manager with a love letter. Part III of this book will tell you what you need to do to get the deal you want.

❖   ❖   ❖

Part III.
Getting The Deal You Want–The Tactics

Chapter 8.
Love Letters vs. Demands

In our last chapter about WIIFMs, I indicated that successful negotiators leverage their knowledge of basic human nature; they realize that a hiring manager will tend to respond more favorably to a request framed in a way that shows the hiring manager what advantage he or she personally gains from giving the requested item.

In this chapter, we will delve more deeply into choosing just the right way to frame – then convey – our negotiation requests so that the hiring manager can really "hear" us when we make those requests.

Conveying your Wish List

Wish List in hand, you have your WIIFM factors ready, and you are equipped to get your requests to the hiring manager. Let's look at how the majority of my clients have found success in asking for their wish list items with a method that gets results and leaves everyone feeling good about the process. **Here's your "L" in the "AWL About the Law" Proactive**

Negotiation Process: it represents the "L" in my method of "Sending a Love Letter."

In the law, when one party asks the other side for something, it's called "making a demand." The word "demand" sounds harsh, and when you hear it spoken, it just doesn't sit right with most people. Although lawyers may not place any emotion or judgment on the word when it is used with other lawyers, it's not the proper terminology for you to be using with your hiring manager, because I'm pretty sure he or she will have a more emotional reaction to the word "demand."

No, when we speak to our hiring manager, we are going to choose our words very carefully, as carefully as we would for any type of relationship that we treasure and value and don't want to lose. I encourage clients to treat an employment relationship like a love relationship.

Picture the hiring manager at the company as if he or she is someone who has fallen in love with you, who wants to engage in a long-term relationship with you, and who has asked you to marry him or her. So now, by engaging in future employment with the company, you are saying, "I'm in love with you too. Let's get married. And before I say "I do," I just have a few questions about how we'll work a few things out, so I'd like to talk with you about...."

The communication is understandable, and gentle, and done with the goal of building alignment and rapport. That is why instead of using demands, I call our negotiating requests "Love Letters". Because of the nature of job offer negotiations, this type of delicate touch is particularly effective, even in a down economy.

Love Letters vs. Demands

Creating a love letter is much easier said than done. You want these letters to do the heavy lifting for you; by that, I mean, the letter addresses all the "hard-to-ask-for items" that you want and then sets out the reasons why you should receive what you are seeking.

Can you try to do that verbally yourself? Sure, but these can be sensitive conversations to have directly; it can be very difficult to remember everything you want to say, and to say it all exactly right – especially considering the stress of negotiating directly with the person for whom you will be working.

When you take the time to write out a thoughtful request in a Love Letter, the letter alleviates the stress of a one-on-one encounter for *both* sides. It enables you to thoughtfully articulate your position without interruption or any stress. It gives the hiring manager the time to thoughtfully review and then respond to your requests without being put on the spot.

A love letter does the "heavy lifting" by setting forth the objective reasons for why you should get each of the items you are seeking. For example, you can ask for more money based upon a salary survey, or based upon your years of experience directly on-point with the problem the company needs solved right now.

You want the maximum impact, in as few words as possible, so as not to waste your hiring manager's time, or make it look like you are asking for too much. This is much like writing a story for a newspaper or blog where you only have a limited number of words to tell your story. That said, it is a story, so it has to be more than a "tweet," or you risk sounding curt and demanding.

Often times, I "ghost write" these love letters for my clients. This is beneficial because my clients acquire the letter tailored to their needs, yet the hiring manager will never know that they worked with a lawyer. That's part of being a Job "Secret Agent."

There are several reasons why I like this approach. First, the objective of these letters is to build great rapport between you and the hiring manager, and a direct approach without attorneys is often the best way to do that. I recommend people keep their attorneys behind the scenes, unless they are C-level executives negotiating contracts; then attorneys are often at the table starting on Day One. For most other employees, you can always bring in the attorney at a later stage in the process if you encounter a problem or negotiation impasse.

Secondly, when I write the Love Letters for my clients, it helps to send a message to the hiring company about my client's negotiation skills. I want to showcase my client's communication abilities and bolster the company's impression that this person has the executive caliber to succeed and be promoted within this corporation. When you are negotiating your job offer, have no doubt, it's like being on stage – everyone is watching what you do, and how you do it. Every little bit helps.

I often refer to Love Letters as "$100,000 Letters." That amount is what these letters can be worth in terms of where the total value of your overall compensation package starts before sending a Love Letter, and where it can end up over the term of your employment after we send a Love Letter.

You will recall the studies from Chapter 4 that discussed the adverse, long-term financial effects of never negotiating job offers or salary. The book *Women Don't Ask: Negotiation and the Gender Divide* stated that over a woman's career, if she never negotiates her salary, she could lose $1 million. That was reinforced in *The Salary Tutor*, where the author demonstrated how negotiating just a 1% annual increase in salary can add $1 million to lifetime earnings. So, negotiating a better compensation package at the start of a new job not only establishes what you are worth now, it can have a significant impact on your financial future over time.

The books cited above have published studies, and you can refer to them for more scholarly background and information. Because of attorney–client confidentiality rules, I can only describe my work in general terms. I can tell you that the actual dollar numbers involved in many cases can be in the six figures, and deal improvements from Love Letters can be quite significant to clients.

Of course, as we all know, you have your greatest leverage to improve the terms of a job offer when you are going into the deal, so that is when you need to negotiate. You don't want to miss this chance, as you will live with the terms of the deal you negotiate for many years to come.

For example, if next year the entire company gets only a 3% across-the-board raise, you want to make sure you have negotiated the highest possible starting base pay upon which that 3% is going to be based, and upon which the bonus and long-term incentives are going to be calculated, and upon which the 401(k) is going to be matched, etc.

Sample "Love Letters"

The following are two sample Love Letters as part of the "It's AWL About the Law" Proactive Negotiation Process. **Please note: These sample Love Letters are not legal advice, nor should you rely upon them to fit your specific needs. They are merely examples used for educational purposes.**

It is not possible to give you a one-size-fits-all form letter: Each love letter is a unique creation that has to be specifically tailored to suit the personality of the candidate, the hiring manager, and the particular facts of each deal.

I strongly recommend any love letter be crafted in conjunction with your attorney to suit each individual's particular needs. However, these examples will help you get a feel for the general concept, and how to get started to craft the love letter best suited for your particular situation.

In Sample #1, the candidate has a job offer for a marketing role in a pharmaceutical company. He wants to leverage that into an expanded position and title overseeing Commercial Operations and Development, with enhanced base pay, bonus, and equity. He clearly states a persuasive case based on objective comparable data, his expertise, and what he'll do for the company.

In Sample #2, the candidate has a job offer as a plant manager in a manufacturing company. He has more points to make, does so in a very matter-of-fact way that is designed to work for the down-to-earth personality of the recipient hiring manager, and even "gives away" eligibility for a Profit Sharing Plan (for which he was not eligible anyway) to show he is not only asking for things from the employer, but is also willing to make concessions.

You want to remember that your hiring manager is the man with the money (his budget is the source of your paycheck), so he is the person to whom we would have to tailor and specifically personalize any letter. He is also the person who has asked you to enter into the long-term relationship. Therefore, he must "feel the love."

Sample Love Letter #1 – New Job Offer (Pharmaceutical Company)

Dear Mr. Hiring Manager:

Thank you for selecting me to join your team in such an integral capacity. I am confident that my skill set and commercial experience will blend perfectly with yours and will result in us bringing XYZ Company to the next level of success. I am truly excited about the opportunity at XYZ Company, and I look forward to quickly getting on board and making an impact. I know I can learn a great deal from you about how your vision and strategy have successfully grown this company.

To help us make the best use of our time today, I thought I'd take a few minutes to outline for you the following areas where I would like further clarification:

1.) <u>Position/Title</u>. (Hiring manager's name), what I will be doing for XYZ Company draws upon my 20+ years of real-world experience in making new products commercially viable and strategically positioned for success. As you know, I have done this with great success for other drugs, and I am well positioned to do it for XYZ Company.

To get the impact you desire, I will work closely with you and the team to not only handle the marketing aspects of the work, but just as importantly, to coordinate, plan, and launch the commercialization process of all drugs. I will be building the department, overseeing 20% of the sales people and overseeing our product management efforts.

As the senior commercial person in the business responsible for these initiatives, I would have better access to decision-makers in our target organizations if I could present myself to them as the "EVP of Commercial Operations and Development." This makes sense from a reporting relationship standpoint, with me reporting to you as the Chief Operating Officer.

My duties would encompass everything in the marketing job description – and more, as outlined above. Not only is this characterization more complete in terms of what I actually need to do to achieve the success you want, I think it will really help us get there faster and more effectively.

2.)   Compensation. The HR manager (use a name) indicated that you wanted to compensate me at market, so I quickly ran some market comparables to encompass the level of responsibility that I will actually assume in this position.

These comparables, drawn from 10-Ks of other biotechnology and pharma companies within the revenue and size range of XYZ Company, indicate a mean base salary of approximately $270,000, exclusive of bonus and equity.

When I spoke with the HR manager (name), he indicated a salary in the range of $210,000; however, even if I received the full 25% bonus opportunity offered, the salary and bonus total would result in this position paying me significantly less than market, and less than what I was earning in my last position with ABC, Inc.

To try to strike a balance for both sides, I would respectfully request you bring me in at the market mean, with the 25% bonus opportunity (or whatever is the bonus percentage offered to the rest of the senior staff, if that should be greater). I know that I can, and will, be a key contributor to the success of XYZ Company, and that the difference in this salary will soon be insignificant to you in terms of the value that I deliver.

3.)   Equity. Thank you for your offer of 20,000 shares. Before discussing this aspect of the compensation package, I would like to have a better sense of how this fits in with the grants extended to others in the company. My review of the prospectus leads me to believe that recent grants were significantly higher.

I need more information to help me evaluate this, in terms of what portion is a grant, and what are the vesting schedule and the price of my options. Will I have to sign a stock option award agreement, or will all the terms and conditions of things like options, severance, etc., just be covered in my employment agreement?

I'd like to get a head start reviewing whatever I'll have to sign so I can hit the ground running on day one and not have any delays.

4.)   Benefits. Since I am mindful of your time and know that we haven't gone over the components of the benefits package, could you direct me to whomever I should call to find out about benefits coverage, co-pays, eligibility, etc.? In my former positions, a car or car allowance was provided. Will that be a benefit of this position?

I hope this email will be a useful guide for our conversation today. I look forward to successfully closing out these matters and joining your team! See you at 3:30.m. today.

Sincerely,
Your Name
cell phone number

Sample Love Letter #2 – New Job Offer (Manufacturing)

Good morning, (hiring manager's name):

I trust that your recent business trip was successful. I am truly looking forward to joining the XYZ team and working with you! Thank you again for this tremendous offer, and for your flexibility in accommodating the needs of my family and me.

Per our conversation yesterday, the following is a short note outlining what I think is our mutual understanding for moving forward. We've agreed that my start date is to be Monday, May 3. I will meet you as planned in the morning, and we'll go to the facility together from there. I'm truly looking forward to hitting the ground running.

To enable us to have a productive call, and to quickly confirm the final details of our deal, I thought I'd take a few moments to refer in this email to some of the topics we discussed in our last conversation so we can both be on the same page when we speak next.

1.   I am included in the executive bonus plan from my start date, and the written details of the plan will be provided to me upon my start date. In recognition that it will take some time for me to make headway on the initiatives that we've agreed upon, thank you for agree-

ing to guarantee payment of 50% of the target Bonus Plan for my first year.

2.   **[Here's a give-away]** I will not be included in the Profit-sharing Plan until the date that the plan calls for, but my family and I will be eligible for the health insurance coverage effective upon my start date. I have conceded that point, and will agree to it in any written employment contract to codify all the terms of this offer.

3.   As part of the offer letter, the company will provide a severance provision that includes six months of pay and health insurance, and relocation costs back to Denver, in the event I am terminated for reasons other than "for cause."

4.   I've asked my friend who is an attorney to provide us with a definition of "cause" that we can use for our purposes. She recommends we insert into our agreement the following:

Your termination is for Cause if you are terminated because of:

(i) your willful failure to perform your duties to the Company (other than as a result of total or partial incapacity due to physical or mental illness) for a period of 30 days following written notice by Company to you to cure such failure;
(ii) your conviction of, or a plea of nolo contendere to (x) a felony under the laws of the United States or any state thereof or (y) a crime involving moral turpitude;

(iii) your gross negligence or willful misconduct which caused a material financial injury to the Company;

(iv) your material violation of the Company's code of conduct, or the Company's policies concerning harassment or discrimination;

(v) your conduct that caused a material harm to the business reputation of Company; or

(vi) your proven breach of the provisions of any confidentiality, noncompetition or nonsolicitation obligation to which you are subject.

5.   If I am able to sell my home on my own, the company has agreed to reimburse me for the realtor fees in order to help defray the tax liability of the move.

6.   My base salary each year will be no less than $195,000.00. Thank you for agreeing to give me a performance review and consideration for a raise at the six-month point, and on my one year anniversary, and each one-year anniversary thereafter.

7.   I will have three weeks of vacation starting year one. You and I can discuss the need for more time on a "case by case/as needed" basis.

8.   The non-compete will be revised for 1-year, limited to [insert a limited definition of the scope of the business here].

I will provide a list of key contact companies to be excluded from the non-solicitation provision, as these represent pre-existing contacts that I have had for many years based upon my prior experience in the industry.

[Hiring Manager's Name], again this was my understanding from our two conversations. If I've forgotten anything, please advise me or point out any discrepancies.

If you would be so kind as to provide me the employment contract, or a revised offer letter and the non-competition and non-solicitation agreements to accommodate these few points, then we can ink this deal, and I can get on my way!

Sincerely,

Your Name
cell phone number

Risks with Rewards

Remember that these love letters are in fact a form of negotiation. Because we are not just coming right out and saying "I accept," our Love Letters, as nice they are, can be viewed by the company as counter-offers. And we all know about the dreaded Counteroffer Consequence from Chapter 2 – legally, they kill the offer.

So you may ask yourself, "But don't these companies expect us to negotiate?" I can tell you after representing many Human Resources executives over the years that generally yes, companies expect a reasonable amount of negotiations, and are not surprised when you want to negotiate. But you could be unlucky, and be the person who gets an offer "pulled" because he or she tries to negotiate. It hasn't happened to me, but it could happen to you.

Even if a prospective new employer is expecting you to negotiate, you want to present your message to the company in a way that makes them go, "Wow, what an impressive candidate. You know, this person really gets it. He's going to be a solid contributor to my team, and he's going to create value for me. He will have my back. I want this person."

It can be scary to put your feelings out there with a job offer and wonder how the other person will respond to it. Going first is what the hiring manager has to do. Let your love letter ease the tensions of the negotiation process by affirming to the hiring manager that you are on the same page, and are as serious about your new relationship as he or she is.

Send the love letter out to the hiring manager, copying the recruiter and the human resources representative if you have been asked to do so. I recommend clients send the letter as an email, and close the love letter with positive and encouraging remarks, always letting the other side know that further dialogue is welcome.

Help the Hiring Manager Help You

Your love letter is written. In it, you have created your negotiation agenda – all the topics you want to discuss, and the WIIFM factors for each topic that will convince the other side to give you what you're seeking. Now you send the love letter/email to the hiring manager, and plan to follow-up with a phone call in a day or two to discuss the matters in that letter.

Having spent years as a corporate attorney, I can tell you that when a hiring manager wants to hire a good candidate, he always appreciates it when that candidate (or that candidate's counsel) gives him something he can work with to help "sell" the requests to higher management. You can't ask the hiring manager to do that all alone.

You need to help the hiring manger help you. This is your job – and that of your legal counsel. Our love letter gives the hiring manager something he can show to his boss and say, "This is why we should do it, here it is right here – this candidate has hit the nail on the head."

So let's do all we can to help the hiring manager help us. This part of negotiation process can be compared to preparing for performance reviews. You know that you are in charge of keeping track of your performance accomplishments throughout the year and that you cannot rely upon your boss to notice and remember everything you do.

The same principle applies to how you ask for what you want. You can be a great magician, but if nobody sees you pull the rabbit out of the hat, what does it matter? Our love letters have to showcase your talents and indicate "what you can do for the company." That's why they matter – and why they work.

What's Next?

We now have all the components in place for our "It's AWL About the Law" proactive negotiation process: a strategic Analysis of the job offer, a WIIFM'd Wish List, and a well-crafted, persuasive Love Letter.

The next step in this negotiation process is to finish strong. Although you may be nervous about the love letter, it is important to take your best shot, and negotiate from strength in a way that the company will be able to hear you.

Chapter 9.
Getting Past Impasse

Ideally the hiring manager will say "yes" to everything in our letter, and if that happens, you won't need to read any further. But what if you hit a snag and cannot get to "yes" on an item or two? That's when you need some techniques for getting past impasse.

Sometimes you may reach a point where you might think that no progress can be made in your negotiations. This often occurs in labor union collective bargaining negotiations when the parties are trying to hammer out a new contract. When labor unions and management engage in these talks, they negotiate until they reach what is called an "impasse," meaning they are unable to make any more forward progress in their negotiations.

Like two trucks trying to pass each other on a one-lane bridge, neither one can progress without both slowing down and finding a way to work collaboratively with the other so that each can get what it needs. There are actually a number of factors that can lead to negotiation impasse. For example:

- Inability to find common ground with the person on the other side of the table;

- Internal problems within the organization with which you are negotiating;
- Fear of "losing face" between you and your opponent;
- Hiring managers who have poor working relationships with their bosses, or who lack power within the organization to get you what you are seeking; and
- Personality/style differences between you and your hiring manager.

It is your duty to notice these problems and prevent them from getting in the way of your negotiation goals. It is also your responsibility to notice these problems, and cue in to what they are telling you about the power your boss will, or will not, have when you go to work for him within the organization, should you choose to proceed with the job.

You must remember that the key to getting past impasse often is not what you do or what you argue; it is *how* you do it. Impasse sometimes can be caused by the negotiators, not the items over which they are negotiating. It is situations like these where successful negotiators must decide whether to continue the uphill fight, or use one or more negotiation secrets to try to get past impasse.

The negotiation secrets we will address in this chapter are:

1.   Live to Fight Another Day
2.   Find a Next Best Thing
3.   Try the Walk Away

Live to Fight Another Day

Live to Fight Another Day is a technique whereby you realize that when you have hit a brick wall, it is best not to try to bust straight through it. Instead, it is better to take a step back from the situation and let calmer heads prevail. Think if perhaps you can't find a way to get around the wall from one side or the other, perhaps scale over it, or even go under it.

Let's say you and your hiring manager have been discussing what the final terms will be for your employment contract, and due to a number of different factors, you have hit a proverbial brick wall on the amount of your starting base salary. Never one to give up, you remain courteous and respectful, and ask your hiring manager for extra time to get around this impasse by giving the parties time to remove themselves from the table – and live to fight another day – with the following:

You: *"I can see that you feel very strongly about the base salary, and understandably, so do I. I also feel strongly that my skills are a perfect match for this job, and for what you need to accomplish at the company. I know that working together, we could achieve great things. What I would really appreciate is if we could just take the next 24 hours to brainstorm to see if either of us can find a solution that can break this log jam, and that would work for both of us."*

Management: *"Well, you can take all the time you would like. However, we are not going to change our minds. Policy is policy, and we have already done everything we can for you."*

You: *"I hear what you are saying, and I appreciate you working together with me on this situation. I would really appreciate having that extra time, just to see if either of us can come up with a solution. Let's just talk tomorrow at the same time. You never know what one of us may be able to come up with. Thanks so much."*

After that, you either hang up the phone, or else get up from the table, shake hands, and depart. However, just because your discussion stopped for the day does not mean the negotiations are over.

You would be surprised how many times "living to fight another day" results in a successful outcome. This extra time can allow management and you time to break away from the impasse situation.

Now each side can take time to gather its thoughts and think about how it will feel to lose the deal at this stage and over this issue. How far apart are you? What is the lost opportunity cost of not meeting each other at least somewhere in the middle? My experience has been that most often, management will come back with some type of reasonable good news offer for the candidate.

Management wants to feel like a hero in every deal, and we want them to feel that way, too. They deserve the credit for getting you to "yes." To be fair, it takes a heroic amount of time and energy to find just the right person for a job – that person is you – and it doesn't make sense to management to throw a deal away if it can be closed on reasonable terms, even if that means sweetening a deal somewhat. That's way less expensive to the organization than starting the entire search process over again from the beginning, or just moving on to the #2 candidate who isn't exactly right for the job, or with whom there wasn't 100% buy-in.

So during our negotiations, we need to make sure that management gets to feel the way they want and need to feel. Remember that this is a love relationship; you must give a little to get something back in return.

By providing space and time away from an impasse situation, you give management time to save face, and the chance to come back as the hero with the solution to save the deal. This "Live to Fight Another Day" tactic is always worth a shot, and neither party should turn down this opportunity to close a deal successfully.

Your Next Best Thing

Now sometimes, even if you've received extra time, it is not enough to break the impasse. Sometimes the parties just cannot reach accord, and an alternative outcome must be found in order to move forward. In this situation you are going to create your Next Best Thing. This has also been referred to as your Best Alternative to a Negotiated Agreement, or BATNA.

You come up with a Next Best Thing when you decide what it is on your Wish List that you can do without in order to move the deal forward. If you can settle for an alternative, it is better than gaining nothing at all and losing the deal.

You want to ask yourself, how important is this item to me? Am I willing to walk away from the job if I don't get it? Am I going to come back and offer a compromise, or will I just concede the point and accept what the employer is offering?

Let's continue our theoretical situation from earlier in the chapter. You were negotiating your base salary, but reached an impasse. So then you asked for 24 hours to attempt to find a way around this brick wall. Now, it is the next day, and you are back talking with your hiring manager, to see if the company is able to do anything to increase its base salary offer. Let's just say this is a particularly difficult company, and the answer back from our disappointed hiring manager is that unfortunately, he is unable to do anything at this time to increase the base pay.

The ball is now in your court, and it is up to you to offer a compromise. Although this situation isn't ideally what you wanted, you can still make it a step in the right direction, a step toward getting past impasse. If you have decided that your Next Best Thing is to move forward with this job offer, even if you have to take less base pay than is the ideal on your Wish List, then here's an example of an alternative negotiation you could utilize to put you on the right path in negotiations with this hiring manager:

> You: *"I can tell you tried to work with me on this, Mr. Hiring Manager, and I truly appreciate your efforts. That means a lot to me, and it just reinforces that this is the right fit for me, and that together we are going to be a great team. I'm willing to move forward with this. I would ask, though, that you agree to re-evaluate my performance for a __% raise after 3 months because I have no doubt you are going to see that I am worth it. I appreciate that you cannot do it now, but I would ask that you agree to put in my offer letter that I am eligible for an X% increase at the three-month point, and I'll trust you to make your decision based on that."*

Maybe the hiring manager will say sure and agree that very well may be the best course of action.

Does it mean you are definitely going to get that raise in three months? Although it is always my preference to lock in a for-sure negotiated increase, in this case, it doesn't look like that will be happening. But at least you've gotten something: you've gotten the job, and you've secured your boss's buy-in to consider the raise at three months. And as always, remember to get it in writing.

There are many, many options that could be proposed to get past impasse, and this is just one for illustration purposes. When I work with clients, we construct individual proposals that best suit the needs of each client, and the deal, and of course I recommend that approach in every instance.

The Walk Away

There may come a time when you cannot reach an agreement on your contract, when you're stuck at an impasse with no chance for a solution, and when not even a Next Best Thing will work. These are the times when I can recommend you consider using a last resort technique that I call the art of the "Walk Away."

Use the Walk Away technique when you determine that the terms of the deal are such that you cannot live with them, and that it is preferable for you to walk away from the deal rather than to accept the terms offered to you. Sometimes the unfavorable terms of such proposals are called "deal breakers."

The reason this is called a negotiation technique is because you have to ask yourself, "Can I walk away from the deal, and by doing so, cause the other side to change the undesirable terms, and then give me the offer?" The answer can in fact be yes. But there is no guarantee of a yes.

In our scenario above, here's how the Walk Away could have occurred if the Next Best Thing had not worked out. Let's say the company not only rejected any increase in the base pay, but it also rejected your proposal for an increase at the three-month point. In fact, the hiring manager tells you candidly that pay has been frozen for a year, and there may be no pay increase next year either. You now have to make a decision – either accept the job under what you consider very unfavorable compensation terms, or reject the offer. Here's a Walk Away option:

> You: *"You know I really want to work with you and to contribute to the good work you are doing. I have all the right expertise to hit the ground running and start delivering from Day One. I know I am the right value hire for this job. I want to do the work, and I sure hope an opportunity will arise where the company can fit me into its compensation mode so I can say yes and we can have a deal.*
>
> *Until that time, I have to decline this offer under its current terms – and I do so with great regret. XYZ is a leader in the industry, and I've always wanted to work here – and especially to work for you. I respect*

you so much, Mr. Hiring Manager, and it's been my pleasure to meet you. I surely hope the company's circumstances will change, and that you will be able to call me back with more favorable offer terms so that I can join your team one day very soon."

When you do the Walk Away, please do so fully expecting that you will never again hear from the hiring manager. Do not expect he will come chasing after you. Is it possible that he will? Absolutely! But don't count on it. Just expect that you are saying goodbye in a very classy, nice way.

I can tell you numerous instances where clients of mine have had companies get back in contact with them months after the Walk Away to offer them bigger jobs, with greater levels of compensation, after they turned down jobs that were at a lower level of pay and responsibility. That is because of *how* we did the Walk Away.

We left the hiring managers feeling good about the situation: we made them see how much my client liked the hiring manager, the company, and the work, but that it was just this particular deal that was not right. We left the door open to be invited to come back for a "right" situation, should one become available.

I have personally used the Walk Away in new job negotiations, and I will share one of my success stories with you as well. Many years ago, I was interviewing for a general counsel job. Across the table from me were the general counsel of the parent company, the head of human resources, and another high-ranking executive. As I was sitting there, they offered an employment contract for my review and explained that it contained the terms of my employment should I accept the position for which I was interviewing.

After a quick review of the document, I detected that the base salary was significantly lower than I would have expected for an organization of that size and for such a major metropolitan area where the job was located. When I was asked for some immediate feedback, I simply stated, "I would have thought the base salary would have been higher for a position of this level." This is when the human resources VP stated, as if reading from a script, "We have done independent research, and we have found that this is the right salary range for a position of this level in this metropolitan market."

Now you may be thinking, "What do you do, Robin?" First, you look at where the leverage is in the deal – organization or candidate. In this case, I was employed elsewhere and did not need to relocate for this job. The organization had a greater need to immediately fill the position. Clearly, compensation was the key term in the deal, and since we were very far apart on that, it fell into the category of "deal breaker." The manner in which the VP of HR presented the alleged survey results could have been interpreted rather negatively, if I chose to take it that way.

However, no matter how offended you may feel by what the organization says to you, your objective is not to burn bridges. My general rule is to presume that no one is trying to be offensive or insulting, even if you emotionally react to it that way. In the course of negotiations, I have heard things done or said that make me shake my head and wonder "what the heck?" I just ask you to let it go. Take a deep breath and press on as if no one means to say or do anything that is the least bit offensive to you.

Your first decision tree is, do I want this deal? If yes, then you engage in the negotiations dance as set forth more fully in the previous chapters of this book. If you feel that the base salary number is so highly offensive that it truly is a "deal breaker," that you are widely far apart, and you don't need this job, then you may wish to take the drastic step of the "walk away." That is what I did.

In this situation, I simply said, "If you've done the research and you think that you can find someone with the right skills and abilities to do this job in this market for this amount of money, I certainly respect that. And I think you should hire that person, because it would be the right move for the company, and I certainly would expect you to do only whatever is in the best interest of the company."

I continued, "I have so enjoyed meeting all of you. You are a terrific group of executives, and I have a lot of respect for you and for this organization. Maybe at some time in the future we'll have a chance to work together because I surely would welcome that. I wish all you nothing but the best. It's been a pleasure. Thank you so much."

Then I stood up, shook everyone's hands, said goodbye, and walked out.

Sure enough, two weeks later I got a call from the CEO of the corporation. "What is it going to take in order for you to accept this job?" he asked. Eureka! We had broken through impasse, and now we could get into the real negotiations!

Recap: Your Arsenal Against Deal-Breakers

Remember that you always have a few alternatives to getting past impasse. The first is giving yourself the opportunity or chance to fight another day.

The second alternative is to find a Next Best Thing.

The third is the Walk Away.

And of course, while this may seem drastic, you do have a final alternative – to concede and take the deal that was offered. The path you choose to follow depends on who has more leverage in the deal, and what you want more.

Chapter 10.
Completing the Mission

At this point, you have successfully completed the following stages of the job offer negotiation process. Here's how your progress lines up with our AWL acronym. Every step doesn't have a letter in our acronym, nor does it need to, because we can easily follow these simple steps:

1. Analyzed the offer to determine what was good, what was not so good, and what was missing;

2. Created Your Wish List of what it would take to make this the "ideal" job for You;

3. "WIIFM'ed" Your Wish List;

4. Developed AWL Proactive Negotiation strategies and tactics to effectively communicate your Wish List;

5. Written the Love Letter with your WIIFMs, and sent it to the right people;

6. Followed-Up on the Love Letter with verbal discussions, and

7. Moved past impasse on any potential deal-breakers.

There isn't anything left to do except sign on the dotted line to move forward with the job of your dreams, or to decline this one, and wait for the next best opportunity. Mission Accomplished!

I hope you have achieved everything on your wish list, and that you have now signed an employment agreement or offer letter that is everything you wished it would be. I often tell clients that I truly hope the job they obtain now will be the job from which they retire thirty years from now. Yet we all recognize that it is rare in today's business environment that all good things will stay static (or good) forever.

Part of our preparation when we enter into any new job is expecting that like all good things this, too, will come to an end someday. And to the extent possible, I want your job offer and employment documents to protect you in the event of change.

Corporate America is a vast and constantly-changing environment where employees can find themselves cycling through jobs. As time passes, so do jobs, bosses, departments, and corporations. This is how businesses work. And ultimately, no one can control how this cycle will play out.

In the introduction of this book I talked about market forces that can intervene and wreak havoc upon professional careers. These forces can be out of your control as the employee. However, they are a part of life, and a part of how corporate America functions in order to keep its businesses alive.

Your performance at your job may be top of the line; you may love the people with whom you work, and the environment in which you work. However, that is ultimately not enough to control the fate of your company or your continued employment. Mergers and downsizing cause companies to cut jobs regardless of the performance of their employees. Outsourcing, better technology, and new bosses want you replaced by a new information system, a different team, or a cheaper workforce.

Although losing a job through no fault of your own can seem like the end of the world, sometimes our only option is to find a way to make the best out of these tough situations. Many see these changes as times of loss, however when handled the right way, we can reframe our perspective and recast them as times of opportunity.

A Final Word About Success with Severance

Successful transitions are best navigated when you prepare for them in advance. I want to reinforce the importance of trying to negotiate for protective terms – for severance pay and benefits continuation – in your employment agreement or offer letter.

Severance is just another factor to put on your "wish list," but since it is such an important factor, it truly merits some special attention.

To recap our earlier discussions from Chapter 1, "At will" employment is the general rule in the United States. That means either you, or your employer, generally can terminate the employment relationship at any time, for any reason (as long as it's not for an illegal reason, like your age, gender, race, color, religion, national origin, disability, etc.) and neither of you owes the other anything – unless you have agreed otherwise under some type of contract or policy.

Severance is the contractual "quid pro quo" that employees seek from employers as consideration when the employee has been doing a good job and did nothing wrong, yet the company still decides to fire them for the company's convenience. It is not always easy to ask for severance here in the United States because companies are not legally obligated to give at-will employees severance.

Generally, though, there are many good reasons for companies to offer severance packages to departing employees to assist them in making a transition effectively. The most notable reason is to deter employees from suing the company and alleging that the real reason for the termination is illegal or discriminatory. Lawsuits are costly and disruptive. Providing transition pay and benefits to help an employee while he looks for a new job not only shows an employer's good will, but also provides consideration to support a release of claims that most companies will ask the employee to sign, promising he will not sue the company in exchange for getting the severance pay and benefits.

Many employers are learning that employees like to know before they commit to a job offer that severance pay and benefits will be provided in the event they subsequently lose their jobs due to no fault of their own. All senior level executives know that one of the most important reasons you have an employment contract is for the termination provisions – so that you know your rights to pay and benefits upon any termination of your employment.

This is completely consistent with our characterization of the job offer negotiation process as a love relationship. The offer letter and employment agreement are like the "prenuptial agreement" in a marriage; these documents express in a positive way, mutually agreed upon by the parties, how the relationship will unwind should that ever have to happen.

Surely it is not the hope of the parties entering into the employment relationship that any breakup will happen. But market forces beyond the employee's control, and certainly beyond the control of the hiring manager, can intervene and affect the relationship. Agreeing in advance on how you'll dissolve the relationship at some future date prevents either party from becoming disagreeable during the break-up.

This is crucially important under stressful circumstances. A prime example of a stressful circumstance is when the break-up happens due to the love being gone between the hiring manager and the employee – a time when it can be difficult to negotiate for severance if you have zero entitlement.

How do you ask for severance protection? Let's say you have been given your employment agreement; however, you notice that there is no clause for severance pay if the company elects to let you go. Here are a few examples of how to ask about severance if you are put into this position:

First Sample Severance "Ask"

"I am making a commitment to the company, and I trust the company is making the same to me. My spouse and I are willing to relocate and we will put down roots and become a part of this new community once I accept this position. I appreciate the company's desire for flexibility. My question is, **how will the company work with me to facilitate my transition** in the event market forces change at some time and due to factors beyond our control, my position is eliminated; or I am let go for the convenience of the company for some other reason, like a change in management?"

By asking the question this way, it gives the company the opportunity to respond with the first offer – versus you presuming you know what to request.

I once represented a Vice President of Human Resources who came to me asking me to improve the severance package he had already negotiated for himself in his employment agreement. He had negotiated for a six-month severance package as part of his job offer when going in to the job, but once on the job, he learned others at his level had one-year severance pay packages. When he asked his boss why he only received a six-month severance package, he was told, "That's what you asked for." **So, be careful what you ask for – you may get it.**

And if you don't know what the company is willing to offer, instead of presuming you know what the "right" amount is to request, consider just asking the question first, like in my example above, and see what the company offers as step one. Then we can always go back and negotiate for more, using our WIIFM techniques.

You may be thinking that as a new employee, you may not have the leverage to already begin discussions of what will happen in the event of your termination. But remember – the key to success with severance is the way you **ask.**

Severance is the consideration you seek in exchange for at-will employment. By asking, "how the company will work with you" during these times caused by events that are out of your control, you are looking out for yourself in the future.

Second Sample Severance "Ask"

Another basis for initiating the severance discussion can be around the company asking you to sign a non-competition or non-solicitation agreement that restricts your ability to earn a living after your employment is terminated for any reason. A sample WIIFM factor here can be as follows:

> "I understand that the company believes that it needs to restrict my ability to earn a living post-termination, and I can respect some of those concerns. Can you help me understand how the company will work with me to help me honor those obligations to protect the company, while at the same time enabling me to remain financially whole and able to take care of my obligations to provide for my family while in transition?"

The odds are excellent that the hiring manager with whom you are having these conversations has been "downsized" himself at least once, too. Any company should understand that these situations are a very common reality, and that severance is something that the savvy employee definitely discusses as part of job negotiations.

Apply the negotiation secrets and the "It's AWL About the Law" Proactive Negotiation Process described in this book when negotiating for this important Wish List item.

Change of Control Agreements

A change of control agreement is a type of contract whose primary purpose is to provide an executive with severance pay and benefits in the event his employment is terminated, or his duties or responsibilities are reduced and he elects to depart due to Good Reason, all within a certain time period after ownership or control of the company changes.

The consideration for a change of control agreement usually is that the employee agrees to continue employment when a company changes ownership. In exchange, the employee gets this agreement with the contingency plan provisions – which generally provide a more generous severance package than standard severance pay and benefits – in the event the employee is let go without cause or resigns for Good Reason within some time period following the change of control.

There are complicated rules and possible tax penalty implications applicable to change of control severance. If you receive such a change of control agreement, you should have it reviewed by legal counsel – no exceptions.

Each company's Board of Directors defines change of control, and determines which senior-level executives will receive a change of control, or change in control (the terms are used interchangeably) agreement. You may recall from our work in Chapters 3 and 5 that compensation for the top executives and members of the board of directors of every publicly-traded company in the United States must be reported to the SEC. I explained how you can obtain this information free from the SEC's EDGAR database.

You can check *http://corporate.findlaw.com/contracts/compensation/employment/* to review any number of employment contracts for executives from publicly-traded companies to search for sample change of control and other clauses in their contracts.

What's Next for You?

As you follow your career path, you will constantly run into change, whether it is good change, such as a new job offer or promotion, or not so great change, such as a termination or layoff. All of these outcomes are part of the cycle of life as an employee. Like in the wilderness, the individuals who can adapt to their ever-changing environment will be the ones who will survive and prosper.

You are among those who have the skills for survival. By reading this book you have helped to equip yourself for any difficult situation caused by job offer negotiations, and you have set yourself up for the ultimate accomplishment: successfully completing your mission of getting the killer job offer of your dreams.

In the next book of our series, *How to Keep the Job You Love and Be a Rock Star at Work,* we take a look at the world of work once you are on the job. You did a great job getting here, now we want to make sure you stay on your career track and don't make one of the many possible mistakes that can derail smart people from the career path of success.

Due to my corporate positions, as well as my representation in private legal practice of thousands of employees in all different industries and at all levels of responsibility, I've had a unique opportunity to be strategically involved in seeing who succeeds at work, and how they do it. I've also seen how people get taken down and lose it all. I've seen how careers are built, and how they are destroyed – both by the action or inaction of the individual, or as we say in the law, through a "superseding intervening force," meaning somebody or something else.

If only I could have put all this combined wisdom to work for myself back when I needed it! Since no one has yet invented a way to rewrite history, I decided to come up with a next-best alternative: to share with my readers some of these secrets for success that are often reserved only for the top executives in management.

Readers can put these combined job secrets and wisdom to work for their career success – and do it *now*, while they still have a chance to preserve an upward career trajectory.

Anyone who appreciates how competitive today's economy is knows that just one misstep is all it can take to derail years of career planning and progress. The kind of advice to which I want you to have access is usually reserved for the select few who already know "the game" or can afford hundreds of dollars an hour to buy it.

Now, instead of falling victim to corporate power players, every reader can try to get a fair shot at developing the political savvy to outsmart the sharks at their own game and have a better shot at achieving the success for which he or she has worked so hard.

Work is like a marriage. It requires the same kind of planning, foresight, and commitment. Our readers know that if they have screwed up one job relationship, they aren't doomed to make the same mistakes on the next job relationship, but they really want to be assured of that fact by having a plan in place to avoid the same problem – or at least minimize the chance that it will happen again. They realize there is limited time to attain success, and only so many mistakes they can make and still stay on track, especially in Corporate America.

People self-destruct for a lot of reasons. Some have limited emotional intelligence, or think that "playing politics" is something they'll never have to do. Many times it's because they have no idea that someone is out to get them. Other people are simply clueless to what is happening around them, or how their actions are being perceived. They could use a Job "Secret Agent" to help them out while on the job, and clue them in on the things that they may not be seeing themselves.

That's exactly what my next book will offer you. *How to Keep the Job You Love and Be a Rock Star at Work: The Job "Secret Agent" Book Series, Volume 2* will offer you a real chance to learn from those who have gone before - to attain this type of collective wisdom and career guidance that we all crave.

Nobody wants to screw up or to be a victim at work. Everybody wants to have success secrets and helpful business intelligence resources at his or her disposal, and to be able to take the best shot possible. In short, each of us wants to be all that he or she can be.

If you don't already know it all, then you can certainly learn a thing or two from having your own Job "Secret Agent" at work with you, and on your team. Read on, and learn more secrets that are shared in *How to Keep the Job You Love and Be a Rock Star at Work: The Job "Secret Agent" Book Series, Volume 2.*

To sign up for Robin Bond's email list, and for information on the publication of other books in The Job "Secret Agent" Series, go to:
www.jobsecretagent.com

❖   ❖   ❖

Robin F. Bond, Esq. is licensed to practice law in Pennsylvania. For more information about her law practice, visit www.transition-strategies.com.

Groups of all types and sizes, from the media, to nonprofit and professional organizations, to major corporations, have responded enthusiastically to Robin Bond's public speaking and entertaining presentations on a variety of topics related to the law and the world of work. She is quoted in a variety of electronic and print media, including CNN, FOX News, Time magazine, Career Builder.com, Monster.com, the New York Times, the New York Post, and the Wall Street Journal.

For more information about having Robin Bond speak to your group, write to her at robinbond@jobsecretagent.com or contact her through World of Work Media, LLC at 610-296-7117.

For additional information, visit www.robin-bond.com.

Acknowledgements

I would like to thank all of my wonderful clients without whom this book would not be possible. I also thank all of my friends, family members, and professional colleagues who have encouraged me to find the time and energy to continue to write this book, even when I didn't think I had a minute of time or an ounce of energy left to do so.

A very special thank you to Ryder Harman, my dedicated summer intern, who motivated me, and worked side by side with me, to get the outline created and the words on paper. Without his assistance, this work would not be possible.

Extra-special gratitude goes out to my Indiana University School of Business colleagues Mark Cuban and Leanna Johannes, to whom I am deeply indebted for their support and encouragement.

Thank you, too, to my editors, Kate Early, Ruth Weisberg, and Paris Lynn Flowe. And finally I thank Melinda Emerson and Cathy Larkin of www.WebSavvyPR. com, without whom this book never would have made it to press.